W9-BSE-667

Spring

Recipes Inspired by Nature's Bounty

Time-Life Books is a division of Time Life Inc.
Time-Life is a trademark of Time Warner Inc. U.S.A.

TIME-LIFE CUSTOM PUBLISHING
Vice President and Publisher: Terry Newell
Associate Publisher: Teresa Hartnett
Director of New Product Development: Regina Hall
Managing Editor: Donia Ann Steele
Director of Sales: Neil Levin
Director of Financial Operations: J. Brian Birky

WILLIAMS-SONOMA
Founder/Vice-Chairman: Chuck Williams

Produced by
WELDON OWEN INC.
President: John Owen
Vice President and Publisher: Wendely Harvey
Managing Editor: Lisa Chaney Atwood
Consulting Editor: Norman Kolpas
Copy Editor: Sharon Silva
Editorial Assistant: Katherine Withers Cobbs
Production Director: Stephanie Sherman
Production Coordinator: Jen Dalton
Design: Angela Williams
Food Photographer: Penina
Food and Prop Stylist: Pouké
Assistant Food Photographer: Martin Dunham
Assistant Food Stylist: Michelle Syracuse
Illustrations: Thorina Rose
Co-Editions Director: Derek Barton

Production by Mandarin Offset, Hong Kong
Printed in Hong Kong

Copyright © 1997 Weldon Owen Inc.
All rights reserved, including the right of
reproduction in whole or in part in any form.

First Printing 1997
10 9 8 7 6 5 4 3 2 1

ISBN 0-7835-4606-8
Library of Congress Catalog Card Number: 96-33476

A Note on Weights and Measures:
All recipes include customary U.S. and metric measurements.
Metric conversions are based on a standard developed for these
books and have been rounded off. Actual weights may vary.

WILLIAMS-SONOMA SEASONAL CELEBRATION

Spring

Recipes Inspired by Nature's Bounty

Joanne Weir

Spring

Immature heads of spring's green garlic are prized for their sweet, mild flavor.

S pring opens in a wash of green. In farmers' market stalls, grocers' aisles and garden plots, you will find leafy vegetables, tender shoots and slender stalks to beckon the cook. Shiny, edible pods in shades of emerald rest in mounds alongside more somber-hued prickly-tipped artichoke buds and rows of pale, lime green fennel bulbs.

A broader palette of springtime color is introduced in lustrous-skinned citrus fruits, deep red strawberries and yellow-gold papayas and mangoes. The season's color tones are further borne by blue-gray oysters and pale pink salmon and milk-fed lamb.

In the kitchen, this seasonal bounty needs little embellishment. Asparagus spears are only lightly steamed before being drizzled with a vinaigrette or tucked in a simple cheese puff. Fava beans recast an unadorned broth into a satisfying soup. Strawberries are paired with white chocolate mousse, while blood oranges and mangoes join together in a refreshing sherbet. Even spring lamb needs little more than sweet roasted garlic cloves or a handful of mint sprigs to transform it into a centerpiece for the season's table.

Selecting Spring Ingredients

Spring Vegetables. Greens flourish in the cool, damp earth and gentle sunlight that characterize this time of year. As a result, a wide range of greens, in ever-growing diversity, are available throughout the season. Select **lettuces and cabbages** that appear crisp and bright, with no signs of wilting or browning. Those that form heads should be densely packed and feel heavy in the hand. Swiss chard and kale should have smooth, unblemished stalks and crisp leaves; the young, smaller heads are especially crisp and tender.

Lettuce grows well in this season's mild weather and damp soil.

The **bitter greens and chicories,** such as sorrel, frisée, dandelion, arugula (rocket) and Belgian endive (chicory/witloof), are also at their best when harvested young. Look for dandelion leaves no longer than a sharpened pencil, smaller sorrel and arugula leaves, and slender, tightly closed endive that is nearly white. Broccoli rabe, a newly appreciated member of the sprawling cabbage family, should have fleshy stalks, compact florets and no more than a very few flowers.

Bins of freshly cut tender **shoots and stalks** are another icon of the season's vegetable wealth. Purchase straight, sturdy asparagus that are evenly colored from the furled tip to cut end, and artichokes with snugly packed buds. The bases of both should always appear smooth and unwithered.

Of the delicious edible **pea pods** available now, seek out snow peas and sugar snap peas that are bright green and shiny, feel firm and show no evidence of dryness along their seams. Inedible bean pods, such as those that enclose fava beans and garden peas, should be plump and flexible but not soft. Split open, the walls of the pods should feel moist.

Immature **bulbs,** such as green onions and baby leeks, are pulled from the earth during spring's mild-weather days. The best of them have pure white, moist-looking heads and crisp leaves. When shopping for dried onions, look for those that show no signs of sprouting and have dry, papery skins.

Spring's **roots and tubers** are protected from summer's blazing heat which can turn them woody and sharp flavored. The best radishes are firm and look smooth and bright. Seek out new potatoes with thin, fragile skins, and beets sporting vibrant green tops and unbroken skins.

The finest of the seasonal **mushrooms**—button, oyster, morel, shiitake— are firm, plump, well formed and neither moist nor dried out. Smell them: they should offer a clean, fresh aroma.

Spring Fruits. Only a limited variety of fresh fruits are available in these months. Look primarily for the citruses, which bridge winter and spring, and for the tropicals, shipped in from sunnier climes.

Select **citrus fruits** that have shiny skins and feel heavy for their size— a sign of juiciness. **Tropical fruits**—pineapples, mangoes, papayas—all give off a strong, sweet perfume when ripe. You can test a pineapple's readiness by gently tugging at a leaf from the center of its crown; it should pull free easily. Ripe mangoes and papayas will yield to gentle thumb pressure. Passion fruits are ready to eat when they are deeply wrinkled, and may even have a trace of mold on their purplish brown skins. Like green bananas, they can be purchased when still smooth and firm to later ripen on a kitchen countertop.

Strawberries and fraises des bois are the only two **berries** available now. Seek out deeply and evenly colored, plump fruits with fresh, leafy stems.

Spring Meat and Seafood. Although most varieties of meat and seafood are now available year-round, there are a few notable exceptions. Young, tender spring lamb is a favorite of this time of year; select meat that is pale pink and rimmed with firm, white fat. The gray shells of soft-shelled crabs should appear tender, not mushy, and give off the clean, fresh aroma of the sea. And, when selecting spring's fresh oysters, avoid those with shells that gape.

Look for the first crop of crisp sugar snap peas in late March and early April.

Eggs, in every shape, color and variety, are a springtime favorite.

Spring Vegetables

Cabbage Family

1. Broccoli Rabe
These slender, firm stalks with deep green leaves are topped with small florets. They are prized for their slightly bitter, nutlike taste when cooked.

2. Swiss Chard
The dark green leaves and crisp, white or red stems taste similar to, but milder than, spinach. Also known as chard or silverbeet.

3. Kale
Early spring vegetable with a strong, spicy flavor and coarse texture. Ranges in color from blue-green to purple, yellow to white. Also known as curly kale.

Leafy Vegetables

4. Mâche
French name for small, soft, delicate-tasting salad leaves; also known as lamb's lettuce or corn salad. Available in early spring.

5. Belgian Endive
Crisp, white, spear-shaped leaves edged with pale yellow-green or pinkish red and packed in cone-shaped heads. The slight bitterness, mildest in smaller heads, comes through both raw and cooked. Also known as chicory or witloof.

6. Spinach
Mildly astringent, dark green leaves. Reserve smaller, more tender specimens for salads and larger, thicker leaves for cooking.

7. Dandelion Greens
Cultivated variety of the wild plant. Young leaves are used in salads, while older, more bitter ones must be cooked.

8. Arugula
Young arugula (shown here) has small, round leaves that develop a series of notches as they mature. Their mildly peppery taste and tender texture are enjoyed raw or cooked. Also known as rocket.

9. Watercress (pictured next page)
Principally eaten raw in salads or sandwiches, or cooked in soups. Early spring sees the smallest, sweetest sprigs of this spicy-sweet, tender member of the mustard family.

10. Sorrel (pictured next page)
Lemony, sword-shaped leaves are used in salads, soups and sauces. Perennial plant available throughout spring and summer.

11. Lettuces
Basket includes lettuces and other salad greens at peak in spring, including (clockwise, from top) long, crisp romaine (cos); slightly bitter frisée (chicory or curly endive); red-leaf lettuce; radicchio; oakleaf lettuce; and butter (Boston) lettuce.

Peas and Beans

12. Snow Peas
Pea variety consisting of flat, edible pods and tiny peas. Also called Chinese peas or mangetouts.

13. Sugar Snap Peas
A recent pea hybrid, these plump, edible pods are prized for their sweetness, crisp texture and bright color.

14. Pea Shoots
Tender, sweet shoots plucked from pea vines and sold predominantly in Asian markets.

15. Fava Beans
Available beginning in midseason, this variety of flat, kidney-shaped bean grows in thick pods. When very small, they may be eaten raw, pod and all; more mature beans, in long, thick pods, require shelling and peeling (see page 15). Also known as broad beans or horse beans.

earth to blanch them as they grow). For preparation tips, see page 15.

22. Fennel
The bulblike cluster of stalk bases of a plant related to the herb of the same name, fennel has two annual crops, the second in the fall. Prized for its crispness and mild, sweet anise flavor.

23. Rhubarb
Tangy, reddish stalks resembling celery. Discard any leaves or roots, which are toxic. Served cooked, most often sweetened in desserts.

24. Artichokes
The first of this cultivated thistle's two annual crops of immature flowers comes in spring. Baby artichokes need just light trimming before eating whole; only the leaf bottoms and hearts of large artichokes are edible (see page 14).

Mushrooms

25. Button Mushrooms
Descriptive name for common, cultivated mushrooms harvested when small, with their caps still tightly closed.

26. Oyster Mushrooms
Named for the similarity to the bivalve seen in their fan shape, gray color and moist texture. Wild variety, now commonly cultivated.

27. Morel Mushrooms
Wild, honeycomb-capped mushrooms celebrated for their rich, earthy flavor.

28. Shiitake Mushrooms
Asian wild variety, now widely cultivated. Prized for their rich, meaty taste and texture.

Roots and Tubers

29. Radishes
Crisp, cool and spicy, these roots of a type of mustard plant come in a range of shapes, sizes and colors, including red, white and purple.

30. New Potatoes
Small, immature potatoes harvested while their skins are still thin and their waxy flesh is sweet.

31. Beets
Small specimens of this sweet root vegetable are harvested in late spring. Colors range from red, gold, pink and candy striped to white.

32. Ginger
Rhizome, popular as a seasoning, with cream-colored edible skin and pink tips when young.

33. Daikon
Large, white, cylindrical Japanese radish used both raw and cooked.

Baby Vegetables

16. Tiny immature vegetables—baby carrots and summer squashes such as crookneck and zucchini (courgette)—are harvested in the spring and prized for their tenderness.

Onion Family

17. Green Garlic
Harvested in late spring, immature specimens of the pungent bulb are mild, sweet and aromatic.

18. Green Onions
Mild variety of onion eaten when immature, green stalks and all. Also known as spring onions or scallions.

19. Sweet Onions
Sweet yellow onions such as Vidalia onions (from Georgia), Maui onions (from Hawaii) and Walla Walla onions (from Washington), appear in late spring.

20. Baby Leeks
Spring sees one of the two annual harvests for this mild relative of the onion. Small, sweet baby leeks are often cooked and eaten whole.

Shoots and Stalks

21. Asparagus
Tender springtime shoots in colors ranging from bright green to purplish green to ivory (the latter the result of being covered with

Spring Fruits

Citrus Fruits

1. Yellow Grapefruits
Available from early winter throughout most of the spring, grapefruits, reportedly so-named because the fruits bunch together on the tree in clusters reminiscent of grapes, are enjoyed for their bracingly tart-sweet flavor. Yellow grapefruits, also referred to as white, have pale yellow skins and whitish yellow flesh. A common variety is Marsh.

2. Pink Grapefruits
Pink-fleshed grapefruits, generally sweeter than yellow varieties, may be distinguished by an orange-red blush on their skins. Generally speaking, the darker the flesh, the sweeter the taste, with the Ruby variety grown in Texas among the sweetest of choices. Other popular varieties include the Rio Star, Ray, Henderson and Flame.

3. Meyer Lemons
Juicy, roundish, sweet-tasting lemons, available in spring and into early summer. They are prized for their exceptionally sweet, aromatic flesh and juice and thin, soft edible peel. If unavailable, any regular lemon variety may be substituted in recipes, although they will not impart the same sweetness.

4. Eureka Lemons
Commonly available thick-skinned lemons. Used regularly for their juice and flavorful zest. Another common variety is the smoother-skinned Lisbon lemon.

5. Limes
Available throughout the season but entering their peak in late spring, limes are smaller than lemons, with thin green skins and pale yellowish green flesh. They also yield a more acidic juice than lemons.

6. Navel Oranges
Variety of large orange descriptively named for the indentation in the skin at its stem end. A carryover from winter into early spring, navels have sweet, juicy flesh. Because they are easily peeled and virtually seedless, they make an excellent choice for recipes calling for oranges to be cut into segments (see page 15).

7. Valencia Oranges
This small, smooth-skinned variety, available throughout the spring, is the most common sweet orange. Valencias yield excellent and abundant juice and are also good candidates for cutting up and eating.

8. Blood Oranges
Available from midwinter throughout the spring, these sweet, aromatic, small- to medium-sized oranges are distinguished by the reddish blush on their skins and their sweet, flavorful, deep red flesh and juice.

Berries

9. Strawberries
Widely popular, these deep pink to red, heart-shaped berries may be found year-round, but are at their peak from early spring into early summer. Cultivated varieties vary in size from no bigger than a cherry tomato to large ones almost the size of a small lime. Hull ripe berries by twisting off the leafy tops or using a strawberry huller. Wash only briefly. Overripe strawberries can be puréed to make sauces or ice cream.

10. Fraises des Bois
Also known as Alpine strawberries, this tapered, thumbnail-sized berry variety may still be found growing wild in wooded areas of Europe—hence the French name, meaning "woodland strawberries." Today, they are also cultivated commercially, to be appreciated for their mild, sweet, musky flavor. The tiny red berries have a flavor resembling a cross between strawberries and raspberries; white varieties

13. Bananas

Available year-round from various tropical countries, bananas are routinely harvested when green. Best purchased when hints of green still linger at their ends, they ripen perfectly at home, stored at room temperature. In addition to commonly available dessert or Cavendish bananas, seek out the small, sweet variety known as the Ladyfinger.

14. Papayas

Smooth-textured, sweet and eminently digestible due to the enzyme papain that its flesh contains, this pear-shaped native of the Caribbean is available year-round, but is at a peak of quality and plenitude in spring. Papayas range in size from about 6 inches (15 cm) long to three times that size and can weigh in at over 20 pounds (10 kg). Small varieties have pale yellow to deep orange skin and flesh when ripe; large varieties usually maintain a dark green skin but reveal a flesh that is bright orange. Buy those that are only partially ripe, their skins roughly equal parts yellow and green; they will ripen at room temperature, away from sunlight, within about 5 days. Cut the fruit in half lengthwise and scoop out the seeds and any surrounding fibers before eating dressed with lemon or lime or using as directed in individual recipes.

15. Passion Fruits

Cut in half, this wrinkly-skinned, egg-sized fruit reveals a yellowish orange, sweet, aromatic pulp full of edible black, crunchy seeds. Strained of the seeds, the pulp makes a wonderful sauce for sweet or savory dishes, as well as an exotic flavoring for desserts. The smooth, immature fruits will ripen at room temperature within 5 days; they can be stored in the refrigerator for several days, and the pulp can be frozen in an airtight container for up to several months.

16. Mangoes

Spring sees crops from Florida, the Caribbean and Mexico of this sweet, highly aromatic tropical fruit native to India. The yellow-orange flesh has a soft, juicy texture reminiscent of a very ripe peach. Harvested when still green, mangoes ripen easily at home when stored at room temperature; once ripe, they may be refrigerated for up to a week. To prepare a mango, score the slightly leathery skin lengthwise into quarters and peel it off, then cut off the flesh in two thick slices from either side of the large, flat pit; the remaining fruit should be trimmed from around the pit's edges.

carry a scent reminiscent of vanilla. Considered a delicacy, fraises des bois are often served simply adorned with a sprinkle of sugar or a splash of cream or cassis (red currant liqueur).

Tropical Fruits

11. Pineapples

Pineapples were named by Spanish and Portuguese explorers who likened the prickly fruits, native to Paraguay, to a pinecone. Buy those that have fully ripened; immature fruit will be less sweet and will not ripen well indoors. Fruit grown in Hawaii, particularly the Cayenne variety, generally offer the best quality. Refrigerate the pineapple in a plastic bag, using it within a few days of purchase. To prepare a pineapple, twist or cut off its leaves and cut a thin slice off the base to stand the fruit upright. Using a large, sharp knife, carefully cut off the skin in thick vertical strips. With a paring knife, cut out any remaining woody "eyes" along the sides. Then cut up the fruit as directed in individual recipes, cutting out and discarding the tough core portions.

12. Coconuts

Coconuts are sturdy fruits that keep well. The white meat and the milk that is made from the meat may be used fresh, but the coconut most commonly used in cooking today is the prepackaged meat, sold dried, sweetened or plain, and grated, in fine shreds or in large shards. Look for the latter in health-food stores.

Spring Main Course Ingredients

Meat

1. Lamb

Lamb is the quintessential red meat of the springtime table. Although year-round breeding now keeps it in constant supply, meat purchased in late spring and early summer is more likely to come from younger animals and therefore to have the most tender texture and mildest flavor. A rack of lamb is the descriptive term for a partial or whole rib roast consisting of three to seven ribs. Here, several racks have been trimmed and tied together to form a crown roast. Tender, rich and flavorful, the meat of either the flat or tied racks takes well to roasting. Leg of lamb is another popular cut; it can be roasted, butterflied and grilled, or cut into pieces and braised or stewed.

Poultry and Eggs

2. Cornish Hen

This small American chicken is a hybrid of the Cornish and White Rock breeds, and is also known as the Rock Cornish hen or Cornish game hen. Weighing in at about 1 pound (500 g) each, perfectly sized for a single serving, it is the closest available equivalent to a young chicken, or poussin. Although sometimes sold fresh, the hens are more often available in the freezer section of food stores.

3. Quail Eggs

These delicate speckled eggs, about 1 inch (2.5 cm) long, are available in Japanese markets and with increasing frequency in specialty-food markets. Most often served as a garnish, whether hard-cooked, poached or fried.

4. Chicken Eggs

A time-honored symbol of spring, eggs are nevertheless available year-round in a range of colors, sizes and shapes. Regular chicken eggs are either white or brown, with color playing no part in either quality or grade. Some breeds of specialty chicken, such as the Araucana variety, lay eggs in subtle shades of green and blue; look for the pastel-colored eggs in well-stocked farmers' markets. In the United States, eggs are sold in a range of standard sizes, the most common being

jumbo, extra large, large and medium. For the recipes in this book, use large eggs.

Seafood

5. Salmon

Although salmon is farmed in Atlantic waters, most Pacific salmon is caught in the wild and is sold fresh starting in late spring. A center-cut fillet offers the meatiest, most flavorful form of the fish.

6. Shrimp

Available year-round but especially abundant in spring, shrimp (also known as prawns) are generally sold with their heads already removed but

their shells intact. Before cooking, they are typically peeled and their thin, usually dark, vein-like intestinal tracts removed: Use your thumbs to split open the shell between the two rows of legs, then pull away the shell. Using a small knife, make a slit along the peeled shrimp's back to expose the long intestinal tract, and pull it out. To freshen the flavor before cooking, soak the shrimp in cold salted water for 10–15 minutes, then rinse well with fresh water.

7. Soft-shell Crab

In springtime, crabs molt their shells. Caught before their thin casings harden into new shells, these soft-shell crabs may be eaten whole,

them fresh from reputable seafood merchants who have a frequent turnover of product, and avoid any with open shells or those that do not have the fresh, clean scent of the sea. To shuck an oyster, hold it firmly, rounded shell half down, in a folded kitchen towel and carefully insert the tip of an oyster knife into one side of its hinge. Twist the knife to open the shell, then slide the blade against the inside of the flat, upper shell to cut the flesh away. Remove the upper shell and then slide the blade beneath the oyster in the lower shell to free it completely.

Fresh Herbs

12. Chives
These delicate shoots of a plant related to the onion have a mild, almost sweet oniony taste and go well with eggs, vegetables and salads. Their purple blossoms, especially prevalent in spring, make an appealing garnish.

13. Flowers
Pansies (pictured), violets and other seasonal edible flowers contribute added color and a mild peppery flavor to springtime salads and are attractive garnishes for desserts. Make sure that the blossoms you choose are pesticide-free.

14. Dill
Sweet, feathery dill fronds commonly season seafood, veal, eggs and vegetables.

15. Lemongrass
Sprightly and acidic as its name suggests, this tropical grass is a popular Southeast Asian seasoning. Found in ethnic markets and well-stocked food stores, it is especially good with chicken and seafood.

16. Parsley
A natural complement to springtime's egg dishes, salads, ham and seafood. The flat-leafed variety shown here, also known as Italian parsley, has more flavor than common, more decorative curly-leaf parsley.

17. Thyme
An excellent seasoning for vegetables, fish, and lamb, this herb is also commonly available in a lemon-scented variety.

18. Mint
A traditional seasoning for lamb, fresh mint—most commonly the variety known as spearmint, shown here—also seasons poultry, seafood, salads, fruit and other desserts.

19. Garlic Chives
Variety of chives with a noticeable but still mild hint of garlic flavor. Well suited to poultry, seafood, vegetables and salads.

enjoyed for the sweetness of their flesh and their slight crunchiness. Best cooked by pan-frying or sautéing.

8. Dungeness Crab
Found along the Pacific Coast of the United States, this large, popular crab is prized for its abundant sweet, firm, white meat. Most often sold already cooked. For ease of preparation, ask the fishmonger to crack and clean the whole crab for you.

9. Bay Scallops
Tiny bay scallops, usually about ½ inch (12 mm) in diameter, are commonly harvested in cold-water estuaries from late fall and

winter into early spring. They are usually sold already shucked; look for scallops that appear plump and moist and smell fresh and clean.

10. Sea Scallops
About three times the size of bay scallops, sea scallops are at their peak of season from spring into summer. Both varieties are sold already shucked. Before cooking, remove the fibrous muscle, or "foot," from the flat side of each scallop.

11. Oysters
At their best and safest in cool months, particularly those with the letter r in their names, oysters are plentiful in early spring. Buy

Spring Techniques

MOST FRESH, SEASONAL INGREDIENTS require only light preparation before they can be enjoyed at the height of their flavor, color and abundance. The six demonstrations at right highlight how easy it is to prepare some of springtime's signature ingredients. The season's artichokes are pared of their prickly exteriors, greens are rinsed of gritty soil. Asparagus spears are stripped down to their tenderest parts, fava beans are freed from their pods. Citrus fruits yield juicy segments and the very essence of their flavor, the zest.

Such simple preparations lead, in turn, to simple cooking and presentation—boiling, steaming or poaching, grilling or roasting, or the quick dressing of raw greens or lightly cooked vegetables with a drizzle of oil and a splash of fragrant vinegar.

Preparing Artichokes

Large artichokes must have their tough outer layers and prickly chokes removed before eating. Smaller baby artichokes need only have their outer layers trimmed. Rub cut surfaces with lemon to prevent browning.

Cut off the top half of a large or small artichoke. Strip off the tough outer leaves until you reach the pale green inner ones. Trim off the stem end and peel away the tough, dark green outer layer.

To remove the choke of a large artichoke, cut in half lengthwise. Using a small, sharp-edged metal spoon, scoop out the prickly choke fibers.

Rinsing Greens

All spring greens trap dirt in their leaves and must be rinsed clean. Spinach, shown here, needs particularly thorough washing because it is grown in sandy soil.

Put the leaves in a sink or bowl filled with cold water. Swish the leaves well, then lift out and drain the water. Rinse the sink or bowl and repeat until no sand or grit remains in the bottom.

Preparing Asparagus

The woody stem ends of mature asparagus spears must be removed before cooking. When served whole, all but the pencil-thin spears also require peeling of the tough skin from about mid-spear to the base.

Using a small, sharp knife, cut off the woody stem end of each asparagus spear. Alternatively, firmly grasp the end and snap it off; the stalk will break naturally at the proper point.

Using a vegetable peeler, strip away the tough outer skin of the asparagus spear, starting 1–2 inches (2.5–5 cm) below the base of the tip and cutting slightly thicker as you near the end.

Segmenting Citrus Fruits

Citrus fruits may be segmented for attractive presentations. First, cut off the peel thickly to remove the outermost membrane of each segment.

Hold the peeled fruit over a bowl. Using a small, sharp knife, carefully cut between the fruit and membrane on either side of a segment to free it, letting it drop into the bowl with the juices.

Preparing Fava Beans

Fresh fava (broad) beans are doubly protected—first by their thick pods, from which they are easily freed, and then by the tough skin encasing each bean. Remove the beans from the pod, then from the skins before cooking.

Using your thumbs, press down along the seam of the fava bean pod to split it open. Run a thumb or finger along the inside of the pod to pop out the individual beans.

Blanch the beans in boiling water for 20 seconds, then drain. Split open the translucent skin along the long edge of a bean and pop the bean free of its skin.

Zesting Citrus Fruits

A lively flavor source, zest—the brightly colored, outermost layer of citrus peel—is easily removed with a zester. Or use a vegetable peeler to strip it off, then mince finely.

Grasp the citrus fruit in one hand and the zester in the other. Draw the sharp edges of the zester's holes across the fruit's peel to cut away the brightly colored zest in thin shreds.

Spring Basics

SUGARED VIOLETS

Violets, both purple and white, are seasonal symbols that winter has come to an end. Coated with sugar, they make a lovely garnish for cakes, tarts and ice cream.

40	pesticide-free violets
2	egg whites, at room temperature
2	teaspoons water
2	cups (14 oz/440 g) superfine (castor) sugar

CAREFULLY SNIP off the stem from each violet, then rinse gently and place on paper towels to dry.

In a bowl, beat together the egg whites and water until frothy. Using some of the sugar, spread a thin layer over a large plate. Holding each flower by its base and using a pastry brush, paint each violet on both sides with a thin coating of egg white. Then sprinkle lightly on both sides with sugar. Place in a single layer on the sugared plate and let dry for 2 hours before using.

Store in single layers between sheets of waxed paper in an airtight container at room temperature for up to 2 weeks. *Makes 40 sugared flowers*

CANDIED CITRUS ZEST

Use this sweet-tart garnish on cakes, ice creams and fresh fruit.

2	oranges, blood oranges or tangerines
1	lemon
1	lime
1	grapefruit
3½	cups (1½ lb/750 g) superfine (castor) sugar, plus sugar for storage
¾	cup (6 fl oz/180 ml) water

USING A VEGETABLE peeler, remove the zest from all the fruits, making the longest strips possible. Place the strips on a work surface, pith side up, and, using a sharp paring knife, scrape away any white pith. Cut the zest into very thin strips about 2 inches (5 cm) long.

In a saucepan over medium heat, combine 1½ cups (10 oz/310 g) of the sugar and the water. Cover and bring to a simmer. Simmer, stirring, for 30 seconds to dissolve the sugar. Add all the zests, cover and simmer for 3 minutes. Let cool.

Using a slotted spoon, transfer the zests to paper towels to drain. Place the remaining 2 cups (14 oz/440 g) sugar on a baking sheet. Toss the zest in the sugar, separating the pieces. To store, layer the candied zest in sugar in a covered container in the refrigerator; it will keep indefinitely. *Makes about 1¼ cups (7½ oz/235 g)*

BLOOD ORANGE MARMALADE

This preserve can be made with any other variety of citrus fruit. It is delicious spread on scones, muffins or toast or on toasted slices of marzipan cake *(recipe on page 113)*. To sterilize the jars, lids and ring bands, immerse them in boiling water and boil for 15 minutes.

6	blood oranges
3	cups (24 fl oz/750 ml) water
5	cups (2½ lb/1.25 kg) sugar

USING A VEGETABLE peeler, remove the zest from the oranges, keeping the pieces as large as possible. Place them on a work surface pith side up, and, using a sharp paring knife, scrape away any white pith. Cut the zest into very thin strips about 2 inches (5 cm) long. Measure out ½ cup (2 oz/60 g) of the zest strips and reserve; discard any remaining zest or reserve for another use. Using your fingers, peel off all the remaining pith from the oranges.

Cut the oranges in half crosswise; using the tip of the knife, remove and discard all seeds. Place the orange halves in a blender or in a food processor fitted with the metal blade and process until smooth. Measure out 2 cups (16 fl oz/500 ml) pulp and place in a large saucepan with the water, sugar and the ½ cup (2 oz/60 g) zest strips. Stir well to combine.

Discard any remaining pulp, or reserve for another use.

Place over high heat and bring to a boil, stirring constantly. Boil, stirring occasionally, until the mixture thickens and 1 teaspoon of the marmalade placed on a plate and set in the refrigerator jells within 3 minutes. This should take about 40 minutes. If it does not jell within that time, continue to boil until it does. Remove from the heat.

Ladle the hot marmalade into hot sterilized half-pint (1 cup/8 fl oz/250 ml) canning jars (see note) to within ¼ inch (6 mm) of the rim. Using a large spoon, skim off any foam. Wipe the rims with a clean, damp cloth. Seal tightly with sterilized lids and ring bands. Let cool on a kitchen towel away from drafts. If the jars have sealed properly, the tops will be slightly indented in the center and will not yield a pop when pressed gently. Store in a cool, dark place for up to 6 months. Once opened (or if they have not sealed properly), store in the refrigerator for up to 1 month. *Makes 4 half-pint (8 fl oz/250 ml) jars*

ARTICHOKES À LA GRECQUE

À la Grecque means "in the style of Greece" and refers to vegetables cooked in a mixture of olive oil, lemon and aromatics and served as an appetizer. Artichokes prepared in this manner are great in salads, folded into an omelet, or tossed with pasta, and will keep well in the refrigerator for up to 2 weeks. To use, bring to room temperature and remove from the liquid, which may be reused to make a second batch.

4	**lemons**
24	**baby or 8 large artichokes**
6	**fresh thyme sprigs**
3	**bay leaves**
10	**cloves garlic**
½	**cup (4 fl oz/125 ml) olive oil**
1	**teaspoon coarse salt**

USING A VEGETABLE peeler, remove the zest from the lemons in large, wide strips. Squeeze the juice from the lemons.

Have ready a large bowl of water to which you have added 3 tablespoons of the lemon juice. Cut off the top half of each artichoke, including all of the prickly leaf points. Remove the tough outer leaves until you reach the very pale green inner leaves. Using a paring knife, cut off the base of the stem and then peel away the dark green outer layer of the stem to reveal the light green center. If using large artichokes, cut lengthwise into quarters, and, using a small spoon, scoop out the prickly chokes and discard. If using baby artichokes, leave whole. As each artichoke is cut or trimmed, place it in the bowl of lemon water.

Drain the artichokes and place in a saucepan with the remaining lemon juice, the lemon zest, thyme, bay leaves, garlic, olive oil and salt. Add water just to cover. Cover with a piece of parchment paper and weight the parchment with a small plate that fits inside the pan.

Place over medium-high heat and bring to a boil. Reduce the heat to medium and simmer for 5 minutes. Remove from the heat and let the artichokes cool completely in the liquid, about 1 hour.

Divide the mixture between three pint (16-fl oz/500-ml) jars, cover tightly and store in the refrigerator until ready to use. *Makes 1–1½ qt (1–1.5 l) artichokes*

openers

'Tis a month before the month of May,
And the Spring comes slowly up this way.

—Samuel Taylor Coleridge

Warm Asparagus with Eggs Mimosa

2   **eggs**

1   **tablespoon Champagne vinegar**

1   **shallot, minced**

3   **tablespoons extra-virgin olive oil**

     salt and freshly ground pepper

2¼   **lb (1.1 kg) large asparagus spears**

This signature spring dish works equally well as a simple first course or as a side dish. Pencil-thin asparagus can be used in place of larger spears, in which case you can omit their peeling. Braised baby leeks can also replace the asparagus. Serve with slices of toasted country-style bread brushed with extra-virgin olive oil and garnish each serving with a few Niçoise olives, if you like.

HAVE READY A BOWL of ice water. Bring a small saucepan three-fourths full of water to a boil. Reduce the heat to medium and add the eggs, being careful not to crack them. Simmer for 10 minutes until hard-cooked. Using a slotted spoon, transfer the eggs to the ice water and let cool for 30 minutes.

In a small bowl, whisk together the vinegar, shallot, olive oil and salt and pepper to taste. Set the vinaigrette aside.

Remove the eggs from the water and peel them. Press them through a coarse-mesh sieve into a bowl. Set aside.

Cut or snap off the tough stem ends from the asparagus spears and discard. Using a vegetable peeler, peel the bottom 3 inches (7.5 cm) of each asparagus spear to remove the tough outer skin. Bring a large sauté pan filled with salted water to a boil. Add the asparagus, reduce the heat to medium and cook just until tender, 4–6 minutes.

Using tongs, transfer the asparagus to a double thickness of paper towels to drain briefly, then arrange the spears on a warmed platter or individual plates. Drizzle the vinaigrette over the warm asparagus, distributing it evenly. Sprinkle the eggs over the center of the asparagus spears and serve immediately.

Serves 6

O to break loose, like the chinook salmon jumping and falling back, nosing up to the impossible stone and bone-crushing waterfall.

—Robert Lowell

Salmon Gravlax with Pickled Red Onions and Mustard Cream

For the salmon:

1¼ lb (625 g) center-cut salmon fillet with skin intact

½ cup (¾ oz/20 g) chopped fresh dill

½ cup (¾ oz/20 g) chopped fresh chives

2 tablespoons kosher salt

1½ tablespoons sugar

2 teaspoons crushed peppercorns

For the garnishes:

2 cups (1 lb/500 g) plain yogurt

1 red (Spanish) onion, thinly sliced

   salt

½ cup (4 fl oz/125 ml) red wine vinegar

2 tablespoons Dijon mustard

2 tablespoons fresh lemon juice

   freshly ground pepper

2 tablespoons drained capers

   lemon wedges

   fresh dill sprigs, optional

Scandinavians preserve salmon, caught during their spring migration, in a method that predates refrigeration. The fish is coated with a cure of salt, sugar and dill to make gravlax, from *gravad lax*—"buried salmon."

TO PREPARE THE SALMON, run your fingers along the fillet to check for errant bones and remove any you find. Cut the fillet into 2 equal pieces. Place 1 piece, skin side down, in a glass dish. In a small bowl, stir together the dill, chives, salt, sugar and peppercorns. Spread the mixture on top of the fish. Top with the second piece of fish, skin side up. Cover first with plastic wrap and then with aluminum foil. Weight the fish with a flat 5-lb (2.5-kg) weight such as a brick. Refrigerate for 48–72 hours, turning the entire salmon and herb stack and basting every 24 hours with the juices that have accumulated in the dish.

Prepare the garnishes 1 day before serving: Line a fine-mesh sieve with cheesecloth (muslin) and place over a bowl. Spoon the yogurt into the sieve and cover with plastic wrap. Place in the refrigerator and let drain for 24 hours.

Place the onion slices in a bowl and sprinkle liberally with salt. In a small saucepan, bring the vinegar almost to a boil, pour over the onion slices and let cool. Transfer to a sieve and rinse under running water. Drain well and pat dry with paper towels. Use immediately, or cover and refrigerate for up to 1 day.

Just before serving, in a small bowl, combine the drained yogurt, the mustard and lemon juice and stir to mix well. Season to taste with salt and pepper.

To serve, turn the salmon flesh side up and scrape off the herb mixture. Thinly slice on the diagonal and arrange on a platter. Garnish with the onions, capers, lemon wedges and dill sprigs, if using. Pass the mustard sauce at the table. *Serves 6*

Knowst thou the land where the
lemon trees bloom,
Where the gold orange glows in the deep
thicket's gloom

—Johann Wolfgang von Goethe

Artichoke and Lemon Fritters

1   cup (5 oz/155 g) plus
    2 tablespoons all-purpose
    (plain) flour

½   teaspoon salt, plus salt as
    needed

1½ teaspoons grated lemon zest

2   eggs, separated

3   tablespoons olive oil

    juice of 1 lemon

¾   cup (6 fl oz/180 ml) beer,
    at room temperature

6   large artichokes

¼   cup (2 fl oz/60 ml) water

    freshly ground pepper

    corn oil or peanut oil for
    deep-frying

    lemon wedges

    fresh flat-leaf (Italian)
    parsley leaves

If you can find Meyer lemons, use them in this recipe; they add a more complex, delicate perfume and less acidity than the more common Lisbon and Eureka varieties.

SIFT TOGETHER THE FLOUR, the ½ teaspoon salt and the lemon zest into a bowl. Make a well in the center. Add the egg yolks to the well, beat until blended and then add 2 tablespoons of the olive oil, 1 tablespoon of the lemon juice and the beer. Using a whisk, mix well. Let rest for 1 hour at room temperature.

Meanwhile, have ready a large bowl of water to which you have added the remaining lemon juice. Cut off the top half of each artichoke and remove the tough outer leaves down to the pale green leaves. Cut off the base of the stem and peel away its dark outer layer. Cut the artichokes in half lengthwise. Scoop out the prickly chokes, then cut lengthwise into thin slices. As each is cut, drop into the lemon water.

In a frying pan over medium heat, warm the remaining 1 tablespoon olive oil. Drain the artichokes and add them to the pan along with the ¼ cup (2 fl oz/60 ml) water and a large pinch each of salt and pepper. Cover and cook over medium heat until the liquid evaporates, about 15 minutes. Remove from the heat and let cool.

In a deep, heavy sauté pan, pour in corn or peanut oil to a depth of 2 inches (5 cm) and heat to 375°F (190°C) on a deep-frying thermometer. Meanwhile, in a bowl, using an electric mixer on high speed, beat the egg whites until stiff peaks form. Using a rubber spatula, fold the egg whites and artichokes into the batter.

Working in batches, drop the batter by heaping tablespoonfuls into the hot oil. Fry, turning often, until golden brown, about 2 minutes. Using a slotted spoon, transfer to a paper towel-lined plate and keep warm until all are cooked.

Arrange on a warmed platter with lemon wedges and parsley. *Serves 6*

Each plant is a personality, each kind of herb a fragrant memory for any visitor to the garden.

—Rosetta E. Clarkson

Fettuccine with Cilantro, Mint and Cashew Pesto

⅓	cup (2 oz/60 g) cashews
1	small fresh jalapeño chili pepper, seeded and minced
2	cloves garlic, minced
1	tablespoon peeled and grated fresh ginger
½	teaspoon ground coriander
⅓	cup (3 fl oz/80 ml) peanut oil
3	tablespoons olive oil
2	cups (2 oz/60 g) lightly packed fresh cilantro (fresh coriander) leaves
⅓	cup (⅓ oz/10 g) lightly packed fresh mint leaves
⅓	cup (⅓ oz/10 g) lightly packed fresh flat-leaf (Italian) parsley leaves
⅓	cup (⅓ oz/10 g) lightly packed fresh basil leaves
1½	tablespoons fresh lime juice
	salt and freshly ground pepper
1	lb (500 g) dried semolina fettuccine
	fresh herb sprigs

A refreshing seasonal variation on the traditional basil–pine nut pesto, this sauce is also good with other fresh or dried pasta ribbons or strands. Mint is among the first herbs to push up in early spring. Fresh cilantro, also known as fresh coriander or Chinese parsley, is abundant year-round, ready to add its own pungent flavor to a wide variety of savory dishes.

PREHEAT AN OVEN to 350°F (180°C). Spread the cashews on a baking sheet and place in the oven until toasted and fragrant, 5–7 minutes. Remove from the oven and let cool.

Bring a large pot three-fourths full of salted water to a rolling boil.

Meanwhile, place the cashews in a food processor fitted with the metal blade and process until they form a rough paste. Add the jalapeño, garlic, ginger and coriander and pulse several times until the mixture is again a rough paste. Combine the peanut and olive oils in a small bowl. Add the cilantro, mint, parsley and basil leaves and half of the mixed oils to the food processor and process to make a rough paste once again. Add the lime juice and the remaining oil mixture and process until smooth. Season to taste with salt and pepper and set aside at room temperature.

Add the pasta to the pot of boiling water, stir well and cook until al dente (tender but firm to the bite), 10–12 minutes or according to the package directions. Drain and transfer to a warmed platter. Pour the sauce over the pasta and toss well. Garnish with herb sprigs and serve immediately. *Serves 6*

Come, gentle Spring! ethereal mildness, come.

—James Thomson

Asparagus-Parmesan Cheese Puffs

¼ lb (125 g) asparagus spears

¾ cup (6 fl oz/180 ml) milk

5 tablespoons (2½ oz/75 g) unsalted butter, cut into pieces

¾ cup (4 oz/125 g) all-purpose (plain) flour

½ teaspoon salt

¼ teaspoon cayenne pepper

3 eggs, at room temperature

¾ cup (3 oz/90 g) freshly grated Parmesan cheese

½ cup (2 oz/60 g) shredded Gruyère cheese

Asparagus season lasts from late winter through spring and into early summer. Some people consider blanched white asparagus, grown by mounding earth around the shoots to deprive them of sunlight, to be a delicacy; others prefer the more pronounced flavor of green asparagus. Seek out, too, purple-tinged asparagus, as well as pencil-thin, slightly bitter wild asparagus.

CUT OR SNAP OFF the tough stem ends from the asparagus spears and discard. Cut the spears crosswise on the diagonal into ¼-inch (6-mm) pieces. Bring a sauté pan three-fourths full of salted water to a boil. Add the asparagus and simmer just until tender, about 1 minute. Drain immediately and set aside.

In a heavy saucepan, combine the milk and butter and bring to a boil over medium-high heat. Meanwhile, sift together the flour, salt and cayenne pepper into a small bowl. As soon as the milk reaches a boil and the butter has melted, remove from the heat and add the flour mixture all at once. Using a wooden spoon, beat vigorously until the mixture thickens and pulls away from the sides of the pan, about 1 minute. Transfer to a bowl. Add the eggs, one at a time, beating well after each addition. Let cool for 10 minutes.

Preheat an oven to 400°F (200°C). Line 2 baking sheets with parchment paper and lightly butter the paper.

Add the asparagus, Parmesan and Gruyère to the cooled dough and stir to mix well. Using a teaspoon, scoop up rounded spoonfuls of the dough and place on the baking sheets, spacing them about 1 inch (2.5 cm) apart.

Bake until golden brown, 20–25 minutes. Remove from the oven and, using a spatula, transfer the puffs to a warmed serving dish. Serve immediately.
Makes 36 puffs; serves 6

You know how it is with an April day
When the sun is out and the wind is still,
You're one month on in the middle of May.

—Robert Frost

Green Onion, Thyme and Goat Cheese Tart

1   prebaked 9-inch (23-cm) short-crust tart shell *(recipe on page 114)*

For the filling:

1   tablespoon unsalted butter

24   green (spring) onions, cut into ½-inch (12-mm) lengths

2   heads green garlic or 2 cloves regular garlic, coarsely chopped (optional)

¼   cup (2 fl oz/60 ml) chicken stock or water

¼   lb (125 g) fresh goat cheese

½   cup (4 fl oz/125 ml) sour cream

2   eggs

½   teaspoon chopped fresh thyme, plus thyme sprigs for garnish

salt and freshly ground pepper

You can make this tart with sautéed leeks in place of the green onions: Use the white portions and about 1 inch (2.5 cm) of the green parts of 6 leeks. Cut into ½-inch (12-mm) dice and place in a saucepan. Add 2 cups (16 fl oz/500 ml) water and cook over medium heat until very soft, about 20 minutes.

PREPARE THE TART SHELL, omitting the sugar, and bake until lightly golden as directed.

While the tart shell is baking, make the filling: In a large frying pan over medium-high heat, melt the butter. Add the green onions, garlic (if using) and the stock or water and stir well. Reduce the heat to low, cover and simmer until the green onions are soft, about 15 minutes.

Remove the pastry shell from the oven and set aside. Position the rack in the upper part of the oven. Leave the oven set at 375°F (190°C).

In a bowl, mash together the goat cheese and sour cream with a fork until soft and well mixed. Add the eggs and chopped thyme and mix well.

Uncover the green onions and raise the heat to high. Cook until the liquid has evaporated, about 3 minutes. Stir the green onions into the cheese mixture, then season to taste with salt and pepper. Pour the cheese mixture into the prebaked pastry shell.

Bake on the top rack of the oven until a skewer inserted into the center of the tart comes out clean, 25–35 minutes. Remove from the oven and garnish with thyme sprigs. Cut into wedges and serve warm or at room temperature. *Serves 6–8*

Let onion atoms lurk within the bowl
And, scarce suspected, animate the whole.

—Sydney Smith

Sweet Vidalia Onion Rings with Chili Catsup

For the onion rings:

2   cups (10 oz/315 g) all-
     purpose (plain) flour

1   teaspoon baking powder

2   cups (16 fl oz/500 ml) beer,
     at room temperature

1   teaspoon salt, plus salt to
     taste

1   teaspoon freshly ground
     pepper

4   egg whites, at room
     temperature

2½   cups (10 oz/315 g) fine dried
     bread crumbs

     peanut oil for deep-frying

3   extra-large Vidalia onions,
     cut crosswise into slices ¾
     inch (2 cm) thick and
     separated into rings

For the chili catsup:

1   cup (8 fl oz/250 ml) catsup

½   teaspoon cayenne pepper

1   fresh jalapeño chili pepper,
     seeded and minced

Vidalia onions hail from Vidalia, Georgia, where perfect conditions exist for their cultivation. These large yellow onions, most widely available in late spring, are extremely sweet and juicy. If you can't find them, substitute Maui onions (from Hawaii) or Walla Wallas (from Washington), both prized for their sweetness, or use any other sweet onions. Offer these spicy rings as an appetizer or a side dish.

TO MAKE THE ONION RINGS, in a large bowl, combine the flour, baking powder, beer, ½ teaspoon of the salt and ½ teaspoon of the pepper. Mix well. Cover with plastic wrap and let rest at room temperature for 30 minutes.

In a bowl, using an electric mixer on high speed, beat the egg whites until soft peaks form. Using a rubber spatula, fold the whites into the batter. In another bowl, combine the bread crumbs and the remaining ½ teaspoon each salt and pepper. Stir to mix well.

In a deep, heavy sauté pan or saucepan, pour in peanut oil to a depth of 2 inches (5 cm) and heat to 375°F (190°C) on a deep-frying thermometer, or until a little batter dropped into the oil sizzles immediately upon contact.

Dip the onion rings, a few at a time, into the batter, shaking off any excess. Next, dip the rings into the bread crumbs, coating them evenly and shaking off any excess. Place the breaded onion rings in single layers on a baking sheet, separating the layers with waxed or parchment paper.

To make the chili catsup, in a small bowl, whisk together the catsup, cayenne pepper and jalapeño pepper. Set aside.

When the oil is ready, working in batches, slip the rings into the hot oil, being careful not to crowd the pan. Fry until golden brown and crisp, 1–2 minutes. Using a slotted spoon or tongs, transfer to paper towels to drain.

Arrange the hot onion rings on a platter and sprinkle with salt. Place the chili catsup alongside for dipping. Serve immediately. *Serves 6*

Can words describe the fragrance of the very breath of spring?

—Neltje Blanchan

¼ cup (1¼ oz/37 g) hazelnuts (filberts)

3 tablespoons fresh lemon juice

4 large or 20 baby artichokes

2 tablespoons extra-virgin olive oil

1 very small yellow onion, diced

2 cloves garlic, minced

2½ cups (20 fl oz/625 ml) water

salt and freshly ground pepper

3 cups (24 fl oz/750 ml) chicken stock

1½ cups (10½ oz/330 g) Italian Arborio rice

½ cup (2 oz/60 g) freshly grated Parmesan cheese

2 tablespoons chopped fresh flat-leaf (Italian) parsley

lemon wedges

Risotto with Artichokes

PREHEAT AN OVEN to 350°F (180°C). Spread the hazelnuts on a baking sheet and toast until fragrant and the skins have loosened, 5–7 minutes. While still warm, place in a kitchen towel. Rub the towel vigorously to remove the skins; do not worry if small bits remain. Chop coarsely and set aside.

Have ready a large bowl of water to which you have added 2 tablespoons of the lemon juice. Cut off the top half of each artichoke and remove the tough outer leaves down to the pale green leaves. Cut off the base of the stem and peel away its dark green outer layer. If using large artichokes, cut in half lengthwise and scoop out the prickly chokes. Cut the artichokes, large or small, lengthwise into thin slices. As each is cut, drop into the bowl of lemon water.

In a frying pan over medium heat, warm 1 tablespoon of the oil. Add the onion and sauté until soft, about 7 minutes. Add the garlic and sauté for 1 minute longer. Drain the artichokes; add to the pan along with ½ cup (4 fl oz/ 125 ml) of the water and a pinch each of salt and pepper. Cover and cook until the liquid evaporates and the artichokes are nearly tender, about 15 minutes.

Meanwhile, combine the stock and the remaining 2 cups (16 fl oz/500 ml) water in a saucepan and bring to a gentle simmer over medium-low heat.

Uncover the artichokes, add the remaining 1 tablespoon olive oil and the rice and stir constantly until the edges are translucent, about 2 minutes. Add a ladleful of the simmering stock-water mixture and continue to stir constantly over medium heat. When the liquid is almost fully absorbed, add another ladleful. Stir steadily to keep the rice from sticking and continue to add more liquid, a ladleful at a time, as soon as each previous ladleful is almost absorbed. The risotto is done when the rice is tender but firm, 20–25 minutes total. If you run out of stock before the rice is tender, use hot water.

Remove the rice from the heat. Stir in a ladleful of the stock-water mixture (or hot water), the Parmesan, hazelnuts, parsley and the remaining 1 tablespoon lemon juice. Transfer to a warmed serving dish and serve with lemon wedges.

Serves 6

Spicy Deviled Eggs

6   **eggs**

¼   **red bell pepper, seeded and deribbed**

2   **tablespoons mayonnaise**

2   **tablespoons plain nonfat yogurt**

2   **teaspoons Dijon mustard**

1   **clove garlic, minced**

1   **teaspoon fresh lemon juice**

¼   **teaspoon cayenne pepper**

¼   **teaspoon sweet paprika**

2   **green (spring) onions, minced**

     very small pinch of saffron threads

2   **teaspoons boiling water**

     salt and freshly ground pepper

     fresh chives, finely snipped or cut into 1-inch (2.5-cm) lengths

Eggs are a wonderfully versatile and inexpensive ingredient. Used in moderation, they are also nutritious, being excellent sources of protein and vitamins. Chicken, goose, duck and quail eggs, as well as the pastel-colored Araucana chicken eggs, are abundant in April and May and can bring unique flavors and a fanciful presentation to the Easter brunch table.

HAVE READY A BOWL of ice water. Fill a large saucepan three-fourths full with water and bring to a boil over high heat. Reduce the heat to medium, add the eggs, being careful not to crack them, and simmer for 10 minutes until hard-cooked. Using a slotted spoon, transfer the eggs to the ice water and let cool for 30 minutes.

Meanwhile, preheat a broiler (griller). Place the pepper, cut side down, on a baking sheet. Place in the broiler about 4 inches (10 cm) from the heat source and broil (grill) until charred and blistered. Remove from the broiler, cover loosely with aluminum foil and let cool for 10 minutes, then peel and finely dice.

In a bowl, combine the mayonnaise, yogurt, mustard, garlic, lemon juice, cayenne, paprika, green onions and diced bell pepper. Stir to mix well. Place the saffron in a small bowl and pour the boiling water over it to moisten fully. Let stand for 1 minute, then add the saffron mixture to the mayonnaise mixture, mixing well. Season to taste with salt and pepper.

Remove the eggs from the water and peel them. Cut each egg in half from top to bottom. Carefully scoop out the yolks into a bowl; reserve the whites. Using a fork, mash the yolks until smooth. Add the yolks to the mayonnaise mixture and stir to mix well.

Spoon the mayonnaise-yolk mixture into the hollows of the egg white halves, dividing it evenly. Garnish with the chives and serve at once. *Serves 6*

soups
and salads

How could such sweet and wholesome hours
Be reckoned but with herbs and flowers?

—Andrew Marvell

Fresh Pea Soup with Lemon Crème Fraîche

For the pea soup:

4½ lb (2.25 kg) fresh garden peas

1 tablespoon unsalted butter

10 green (spring) onions, thinly sliced

2½ cups (20 fl oz/625 ml) chicken stock

2 cups (16 fl oz/500 ml) water

½ cup (4 fl oz/125 ml) heavy (double) cream

  salt and freshly ground pepper

For the lemon crème fraîche:

½ cup (4 fl oz/125 ml) crème fraîche

1–2 tablespoons milk

½ teaspoon grated lemon zest

1½ teaspoons fresh lemon juice

  salt and freshly ground pepper

  fresh lemon zest, optional

  fresh chive blossoms, optional

It is essential to use very fresh, tiny, young spring peas for this soup, as the larger ones are starchy. Cooling the soup in an ice-water bath will ensure that it keeps its bright green color. This soup can also be served cold: chill for 1–2 hours, adjust the seasonings and ladle into chilled bowls.

TO MAKE THE PEA SOUP, shell the peas, reserving 8 of the pods. You should have about 5½ cups (1¾ lb/875 g) peas. Set the peas and pods aside.

Have ready a large bowl of ice water in which a soup pot can be nested.

In the soup pot over medium heat, melt the butter. Add the green onions and cook, stirring occasionally, until soft, about 5 minutes. Increase the heat to medium-high and add the peas, the reserved pods, chicken stock and water. Bring to a boil, reduce the heat to medium-low and simmer until the peas and pods are tender, about 5 minutes. Remove from the heat and nest the pot in the bowl of ice water. Stir occasionally until cool, about 20 minutes.

Using a blender and working in batches, purée the cooled pea mixture on high speed until smooth, 2–3 minutes for each batch. Strain through a fine-mesh sieve into a clean saucepan. Stir in the cream. Season to taste with salt and pepper.

To make the lemon crème fraîche, in a bowl, whisk together the crème fraîche and enough of the milk to make a barely fluid mixture. Add the zest and lemon juice and season to taste with salt and pepper.

To serve, place the soup over medium heat and reheat to serving temperature. Ladle into warmed bowls and drizzle with the lemon crème fraîche, dividing it evenly. Garnish with lemon zest and chive blossoms, if desired, and serve immediately. *Serves 4–6*

Wel loved he garleek, oynons, and eek lekes,
And for to drynken strong wyn, reed as blood.

—Geoffrey Chaucer

Green Garlic and New Potato Soup

For the soup:

1   tablespoon unsalted butter

20 heads green garlic, about 6 oz (185 g) total weight and ½–1 inch (12 mm–2.5 cm) in diameter at root end

8   cups (64 fl oz/2 l) chicken stock

1½ lb (750 g) red new potatoes, peeled and quartered

¼   cup (2 fl oz/60 ml) heavy (double) cream

2   tablespoons white wine vinegar

    salt and freshly ground pepper

For the garnish:

1½ tablespoons extra-virgin olive oil

3   heads green garlic, ½–1 inch (12 mm–2.5 cm) in diameter at root end, bulbs minced

2   tablespoons chopped fresh flat-leaf (Italian) parsley

    salt and freshly ground pepper

Green garlic is simply immature garlic—the bulb before it forms its characteristic cloves and the papery sheaths that enclose them. Milder in flavor than its adult counterpart, it resembles a baby leek or green (spring) onion with its long green tops and pale green or white bulb sometimes streaked with pink. Look for it at specialty markets in early spring, or substitute 1 clove of mature garlic for every head of green garlic.

TO MAKE THE SOUP, in a soup pot over low heat, melt the butter. Coarsely chop the garlic bulbs and add them to the pot along with ½ cup (4 fl oz/125 ml) of the chicken stock. Cover and cook until the garlic is soft, about 20 minutes. Add the potatoes and the remaining 7½ cups (60 fl oz/1.75 l) chicken stock and raise the heat to medium-high. Simmer, covered, until the potatoes are soft, about 20 minutes. Remove from the heat and let cool slightly.

Using a blender and working in batches, purée the soup on high speed until smooth, 3–4 minutes for each batch. Strain the purée through a fine-mesh sieve into a clean saucepan. Stir in the cream and vinegar, mixing well. Season to taste with salt and pepper.

To make the garnish, in a small saucepan over low heat, warm the olive oil. Add the minced green garlic and sauté, stirring constantly, until soft, about 2 minutes. Do not let the garlic turn golden. Remove from the heat and let cool for 10 minutes. Stir in the parsley, mixing well, and season to taste with salt and pepper.

Just before the garnish is ready, place the soup over medium heat and reheat to serving temperature. Ladle into warmed bowls and distribute the garnish evenly among the bowls, drizzling it over the tops. Serve immediately.

"Meichel in beichel"
A wonderful taste in your stomach

—Yiddish Proverb

4	**eggs**
3	**tablespoons vegetable oil**
1	**cup (5 oz/155 g) matzo meal**
2	**tablespoons chopped fresh flat-leaf (Italian) parsley**
¼	**cup (⅓ oz/10 g) chopped fresh cilantro (fresh coriander)**
½	**teaspoon kosher salt**
⅛	**teaspoon freshly ground pepper**
2–4	**tablespoons seltzer water or club soda**
6	**cups (48 fl oz/1.5 l) chicken stock**
8	**slices fresh ginger, each about ¼ inch (6 mm) thick**
1	**leek, including 1 inch (2.5 cm) of green, cut into ½-inch (12-mm) dice and carefully rinsed**
2	**tablespoons finely snipped fresh chives or garlic chives**

Matzo Ball Soup

Passover, the most widely observed Jewish holiday, commemorates the exodus of Jews from Egypt. It falls on the first full moon of early spring, and the first evening is celebrated with a Seder, a ceremonial meal at which chicken soup with matzo balls is traditionally served. Seltzer water or chicken stock is used to bind the dumplings, with the seltzer yielding a lighter result.

IN A BOWL, whisk together the eggs and vegetable oil. Stir in the matzo meal, parsley, cilantro, salt and pepper. Add 2 tablespoons seltzer or soda water and stir to form a slightly sticky mixture. If it is too dry, add 1–2 additional tablespoons seltzer or soda water. Cover the bowl with plastic wrap and refrigerate until cold, about 2 hours.

Bring a large soup pot three-fourths full of salted water to a boil, then reduce the heat to a simmer. Form the matzo mixture into balls 1 inch (2.5 cm) in diameter. You should have 12 balls in all. Drop the balls into the simmering water and cook, uncovered, until they rise to the top and are cooked all the way through, 30–40 minutes. To see if they are ready, cut into one; the color and texture should be consistent throughout. Using a slotted spoon, transfer the matzo balls to a baking sheet. Set aside.

In a saucepan over medium-high heat, combine the chicken stock and ginger and bring to a simmer. Reduce the heat to medium-low, add the leek and simmer, uncovered, until tender, about 10 minutes. Discard the ginger.

Add the matzo balls to the simmering stock and reheat for 3 minutes. Ladle the soup into warmed bowls, placing 2 matzo balls in each bowl. Garnish with the chives or garlic chives and serve immediately. *Serves 6*

Beautiful Soup! Who cares for fish, game or any other dish?
Who would not give all else for two pennyworth only of beautiful soup?

—Lewis Carroll

Sorrel Soup with Torn Croutons

For the torn croutons:

¼   lb (125 g) day-old country-style sourdough bread, crusts removed

3   tablespoons unsalted butter, melted

    salt and freshly ground pepper

For the soup:

2   tablespoons unsalted butter

2   yellow onions, chopped

9   oz (280 g) young, tender sorrel leaves, stems removed

1¼ lb (625 g) red new potatoes, peeled and thinly sliced

2   cups (16 fl oz/500 ml) chicken or vegetable stock

4   cups (32 fl oz/1 l) water

½   cup (4 fl oz/125 ml) heavy (double) cream

    salt and freshly ground pepper

Sorrel has a sharp, acidic flavor, so it should come as no surprise that its name derives from the archaic French *sur*, meaning "sour." The leaves resemble those of spinach and arugula (rocket) and, like the latter, are often classified as herbs. The plant thrives in the coolness of early spring, when its young leaves have their most delicate taste and tender texture.

TO MAKE THE CROUTONS, preheat an oven to 400°F (200°C). Tear the bread into ½-inch (12-mm) pieces and place on a baking sheet. Drizzle the butter over the bread, sprinkle with salt and pepper and toss to coat evenly. Bake until golden and crisp, 10–15 minutes. Remove from the oven and let cool. Store in an airtight container at room temperature until ready to use. (The croutons can be made up to 1 day in advance.)

To make the soup, in a soup pot over medium heat, melt the butter. Add the onions and sauté, stirring, until soft, about 10 minutes. Add the sorrel and cook, stirring, until wilted, about 2 minutes. Raise the heat to high, add the potatoes, stock and water and bring to a boil. Reduce the heat to medium-low, cover and simmer until the potatoes are soft, 15–20 minutes. Remove from the heat and let cool slightly.

Using a blender and working in batches, purée the soup on high speed until smooth, 3–4 minutes for each batch. Strain the purée through a fine-mesh sieve into a clean saucepan. Stir in the cream, mixing well. Season to taste with salt and pepper.

To serve, place the soup over medium heat and reheat to serving temperature. Ladle the soup into warmed bowls, garnish with the croutons and serve immediately. *Serves 6*

The bean is a graceful, confiding, engaging
vine; but you never can put beans into poetry,
nor into the highest sort of prose.

—Charles Dudley Warner

Fava Bean and Farfalle Soup

2½   **lb (1.25 kg) fava (broad) beans in the pod, shelled**

9   **cups (2¼ qt/2.25 l) chicken stock**

6   **oz (185 g) dried farfalle pasta**

1   **tablespoon fresh lemon juice**

   salt and freshly ground pepper

½   **cup (2 oz/60 g) freshly grated Parmesan cheese**

Around the world, fava beans are a favorite centerpiece of spring feasts. In southern France, the spring fava harvest is a time of celebration. And when April arrives at Chez Panisse restaurant in Berkeley, California, favas appear in many dishes, especially soups and pastas. Don't be put off by the peeling process: the flavor and texture merit the bit of extra effort.

BRING A POT three-fourths full of water to a boil. Add the fava beans and blanch for 20 seconds. Drain and let cool. Split open the skin of each bean along its edge and slip the bean from the skin. Discard the skins.

In a large pot, bring the chicken stock to a boil. Add the farfalle and cook until al dente (tender but firm to the bite), 10–12 minutes or according to the package directions. Add the fava beans and lemon juice. Season to taste with salt and pepper.

Ladle the soup into warmed bowls and serve immediately. Pass the Parmesan cheese at the table. *Serves 6*

18 **small oysters in the shell or bottled shucked oysters**

2 **tablespoons unsalted butter**

1 **yellow onion, coarsely chopped**

5 **large leeks, including 2 inches (5 cm) of green, coarsely chopped and carefully rinsed**

5 **celery stalks, coarsely chopped**

3 **bottles (8 fl oz/250 ml each) clam juice**

3 **cups (24 fl oz/750 ml) water**

½ **cup (4 fl oz/125 ml) heavy (double) cream**

1–2 **teaspoons fresh lemon juice**

salt and freshly ground pepper

Celery, Leek and Oyster Bisque

Oysters are best when harvested in cool weather—in months that include an *r*—so look for them in March and April. Their subtle richness pairs well with the crisp flavors of celery and leeks in this refreshing spring soup. Garnish with deep-fried shreds of thinly sliced leek or the tender, leafy tops of celery stalks.

IF USING OYSTERS IN THE SHELL, shuck them, reserving their liquor; see page 13 for shucking directions. Cover and refrigerate the oysters, then strain the liquor and set aside. If using bottled oysters, strain the oysters from the liquor, then set the liquor aside and refrigerate the oysters.

In a soup pot over medium-low heat, melt the butter. Add the onion, leeks and celery and sauté, stirring occasionally, until the vegetables are soft, about 20 minutes. Add the clam juice, water and reserved oyster liquor. Raise the heat to high and bring to a boil. Reduce the heat to medium and simmer, uncovered, until the vegetables are very soft, about 30 minutes. Remove from the heat and let cool slightly.

Using a blender and working in batches, purée the soup on high speed until smooth, 3–4 minutes for each batch. Strain the purée through a fine-mesh sieve into a clean saucepan.

Place the pan over medium heat. Add the reserved oysters, cream and lemon juice and bring to a gentle simmer. Simmer, uncovered, until the oysters are slightly firm to the touch and opaque and their edges curl slightly, 1–2 minutes. Season to taste with salt and pepper.

Ladle the soup into warmed bowls and serve immediately. *Serves 6*

Oh see how thick the goldcup flowers
Are lying in field and lane,
With dandelions to tell the hours
That never are told again.

—A. E. Housman

Dandelion Greens, Goat Cheese and Walnut Salad

½   **cup (2 oz/60 g) walnuts**

2   **tablespoons red wine vinegar**

3   **tablespoons extra-virgin olive oil**

1   **teaspoon walnut or hazelnut oil**

    salt and freshly ground pepper

2   **bunches young, tender dandelion greens, tough stems removed**

¼   **lb (125 g) fresh goat cheese, crumbled**

The time to pick dandelion greens is in the early spring, when they are still tender shoots less than 5 inches (13 cm) high. The older and taller the leaves, the more bitter the flavor. If dandelion greens cannot be found, arugula (rocket) or mixed salad leaves may replace them in this recipe. Crumbled crisp bacon and garlic croutons make nice additions.

PREHEAT AN OVEN to 350°F (180°C). Spread the walnuts on a baking sheet and toast in the oven until lightly browned and fragrant, 5–7 minutes. Remove from the oven, let cool and chop coarsely.

To make the dressing, in a small bowl, whisk together the vinegar, olive oil, walnut or hazelnut oil and salt and pepper to taste. Set aside.

Rinse the dandelion greens and dry thoroughly. Place in a serving bowl.

To serve, add the walnuts to the dandelion greens and toss to combine. Drizzle with the dressing and toss again to coat the ingredients evenly. Sprinkle with the goat cheese and serve immediately. *Serves 4–6*

The sense of taste can only be restored by a constant diet of unwilted vegetables and freshly picked fruit.

—Hannah Rion

Watercress, Grapefruit and Papaya Salad

2	**grapefruits, white, yellow or pink**
1	**papaya, about 1 lb (500 g)**
2	**tablespoons fresh grapefruit juice**
1½	**tablespoons white wine vinegar**
2	**tablespoons extra-virgin olive oil**
	salt and freshly ground pepper
1	**bunch watercress, tough stems removed and carefully rinsed**

All three ingredients featured here flourish during spring, but watercress in particular loves the cool, moist ground that only this season brings. Often found growing along the banks of streams or brooks, watercress has a distinctive peppery taste that goes well with the sweetness and acidity of grapefruit and papaya, while its dark green leaves contrast prettily with their warm colors.

INTO A SMALL BOWL, grate enough zest from 1 grapefruit to measure 1 teaspoon. Set aside.

Using a sharp knife, cut a thick slice off the top and bottom of each grapefruit to reveal the flesh. Then, standing each grapefruit upright on a cutting surface, cut off the peel and white membrane in thick, wide strips. Cut the grapefruit crosswise into slices ¼ inch (6 mm) thick and then cut each slice into quarters. Place in a bowl and set aside.

Peel the papaya and cut in half through the stem end. Scoop out the seeds and discard. Cut crosswise into slices ¼ inch (6 mm) thick. Place in the bowl with the grapefruit slices.

To the bowl containing the grapefruit zest, add the grapefruit juice, vinegar and olive oil to make a dressing. Whisk together, then season to taste with salt and pepper.

To serve, place the watercress in a serving bowl and drizzle with the dressing. Top with the grapefruit and papaya slices. Toss lightly and serve immediately. *Serves 4–6*

To get the best results you must talk to your vegetables.

—Charles, Prince of Wales

Fennel, Radish and Parsley Salad

2   **fennel bulbs**

1   **small bunch fresh flat-leaf (Italian) parsley, stems removed and leaves minced, plus parsley sprigs for garnish**

12   **radishes, trimmed and cut into paper-thin slices**

3   **tablespoons extra-virgin olive oil**

2   **tablespoons fresh lemon juice**

1   **clove garlic, minced**

   salt and freshly ground pepper

   lemon wedges

Radish, with its pungent bite, and fresh-tasting parsley find a perfect companion in fennel, with its hint of licorice flavor. Fennel's name comes from the Latin for "little hay," probably describing its feathery green foliage.

CUT OFF THE FEATHERY TOPS and stems from the fennel bulbs and discard. Trim away any yellowed or bruised outer leaves and then cut each bulb in half through the stem end. Cut out the tough core portion and place the halves, cut side down, on a work surface. Using a sharp knife, cut the fennel crosswise into paper-thin slices. Place the slices in a bowl. Add the parsley and radishes and toss well to mix. Set aside.

To make the dressing, in a small bowl, whisk together the olive oil, lemon juice, garlic and salt and pepper to taste.

To serve, drizzle the dressing over the salad and toss to coat the ingredients evenly. Transfer to a serving bowl, garnish with lemon wedges and parsley sprigs and serve immediately. *Serves 6*

For lo, the winter is past, the rain is over and gone;
The flowers appear on the earth, the time of singing has come

—Song of Solomon

Sugar Snap Pea and Mint Salad

1½ **lb (750 g) sugar snap peas, ends trimmed**

1   **tablespoon Champagne vinegar**

1   **small shallot, minced**

3   **tablespoons extra-virgin olive oil**

     salt and freshly ground pepper

¼   **cup (¼ oz/7 g) fresh mint leaves, cut into thin strips, plus mint sprigs for garnish**

Fresh peas and mint are natural partners and are often paired in hot side dishes and soups. This version of the classic combination, featuring spring's sugar snap peas rather than the more traditional garden peas, appeals to the season's celebration of fresh, light flavors. Thin strips of prosciutto can be added for a more robust taste. Serve this versatile salad to open a meal or to accompany a main course of grilled lamb.

HAVE READY A BOWL of ice water. Bring a large saucepan three-fourths full of salted water to a boil. Add the sugar snap peas and simmer until bright green and almost tender, 1½–2 minutes. Drain immediately and transfer to the ice water to halt the cooking. Let stand for 5 minutes, then drain and set aside.

To make the dressing, in a small bowl, whisk together the vinegar, shallot, olive oil and salt and pepper to taste.

To serve, place the sugar snap peas and thin strips of mint in a bowl and drizzle with the dressing. Toss to coat the ingredients evenly. Transfer to a serving bowl and garnish with mint sprigs. Serve immediately, arranging the salad attractively on each plate, if desired. *Serves 4–6*

Ho! 'tis the time of salads.

—Laurence Sterne

½ cup (2 oz/60 g) pecan halves

4 heads Belgian endive
   (chicory/witloof)

1 large bunch arugula (rocket),
   tough stems removed

3 blood oranges

1 teaspoon walnut or
   hazelnut oil

2 tablespoons extra-virgin
   olive oil

1 tablespoon sherry vinegar
   or Champagne vinegar

   salt and freshly ground
   pepper

Belgian Endive, Arugula and Blood Orange Salad

Arugula, which grows best in the cooler temperatures of spring and autumn, has a flavor that brings to mind pepper, mustard and horseradish. It is an excellent component of salads that contrast its tangy character with sweet ingredients such as blood oranges and rich components such as walnut oil. Garnish each serving with a sprinkling of blood orange zest, if you like.

PREHEAT AN OVEN to 350°F (180°C). Spread the pecans on a baking sheet and place in the oven until toasted and fragrant, 5–7 minutes. Let cool.

Trim off 1 inch (2.5 cm) from the stem end of each endive and separate the leaves into individual spears. Rinse the endive and arugula leaves and dry thoroughly. Place them in a large bowl, cover with a damp towel and refrigerate until serving, or for up to 3 hours.

Grate enough zest from 1 orange to measure ½ teaspoon; set aside. Using a sharp knife, cut a thick slice off the top and bottom of each orange to reveal the flesh. Then, standing each orange upright on a cutting surface, cut off the peel and white membrane in thick, wide strips. Working with 1 orange at a time, hold the orange over a bowl and cut along either side of each segment between the membrane and flesh to free the segments from the membrane. As the segments are freed, let them drop into the bowl. When all are removed, squeeze the membrane to release as much juice as possible into the bowl. Using a slotted spoon, transfer the orange segments to a serving bowl and remove any seeds. Set aside. (You should have about 2 tablespoons juice remaining in the bowl.)

To the bowl containing the orange juice, add the walnut or hazelnut oil, olive oil, sherry or Champagne vinegar, and reserved orange zest. Whisk together, then season to taste with salt and pepper.

To serve, add the endives and arugula to the orange segments. Drizzle with the dressing and scatter on the pecans. Toss well and serve. *Serves 4–6*

main
courses

The mountain sheep are sweeter,
But the valley sheep are fatter;
We therefore deemed it meeter
To carry off the latter.

—Thomas Love Peacock

Rack of Spring Lamb with Roasted Garlic

2	heads garlic
2½	tablespoons olive oil
¼	cup (2 fl oz/60 ml) water
3	tablespoons whole-grain mustard
2	tablespoons fresh lemon juice
½	teaspoon salt, plus salt to taste
½	teaspoon freshly ground pepper, plus pepper to taste
1½	cups (3 oz/90 g) fresh white bread crumbs
3	racks of lamb, about 1½ lb (750 g) each, trimmed of excess fat
2	tablespoons unsalted butter, melted

For this recipe, you (or your butcher) must first "french" the racks: Trim off 2 inches (5 cm) of fat and membrane between the ribs to expose the tips of the bones, then cut through the backbone between the ribs to make carving easier. Fresh spring vegetables, such as asparagus, baby carrots and new potatoes, make a delicious accompaniment.

PREHEAT AN OVEN to 400°F (200°C). Discard the excess papery sheath from the garlic heads and place in a small baking dish. Drizzle with ½ tablespoon of the olive oil and the water. Cover with aluminum foil and bake until soft, about 45 minutes. Let cool slightly. Leave the oven set at 400°F (200°C).

Separate the garlic cloves and squeeze the pulp from the skins into a small bowl; discard the skins. Whisk in the remaining 2 tablespoons olive oil, the mustard, lemon juice and ½ teaspoon each salt and pepper. In another bowl, season the bread crumbs with salt and pepper to taste.

Lay the racks of lamb in a roasting pan side by side and fat side up. Roast for 10 minutes. Remove from the oven and immediately rub the garlic mixture over the fat side of each rack. Then spread the bread crumb mixture over the garlic mixture. Drizzle with the melted butter and return the lamb to the oven. Continue to roast until the crumbs are lightly golden and an instant-read thermometer inserted into the thickest portion of a rack away from the bone registers 130°–135°F (54°–57°C) for medium-rare, or the meat is pink when cut into with a sharp knife, about 25 minutes longer. Remove from the oven, cover with aluminum foil and let rest for 10 minutes.

Preheat a broiler (griller). Uncover and place the roasting pan under the broiler about 5–6 inches (13–15 cm) from the heat source. Broil (grill) the lamb racks until the crumbs are deep golden brown, 30–60 seconds.

To serve, place the racks on a cutting board and slice between the ribs. Arrange 2 or 3 ribs on each warmed individual plate. *Serves 6*

Serenely full, the epicure would say,
Fate cannot harm me, I have dined today.

—Sydney Smith

Pork Chops with Morels and Thyme

½   **cup (4 fl oz/125 ml) boiling water**

¼   **oz (7 g) dried morel mushrooms or other dried wild mushrooms**

2   **teaspoons vegetable oil**

6   **center-cut pork chops, each about 6 oz (185 g) and 1 inch (2.5 cm) thick, trimmed of excess fat**

     salt and freshly ground pepper

2   **teaspoons unsalted butter**

½   **lb (250 g) fresh morel or other fresh wild or cultivated mushrooms, trimmed and brushed clean** *(see note)*

1½   **cups (12 fl oz/375 ml) chicken stock**

1   **teaspoon chopped fresh thyme, plus thyme sprigs for garnish**

Morels signify spring for mushroom lovers. Thin fleshed, spongy and brown, these wild mushrooms have a delicate, earthy, nutty flavor. To clean their honeycombed ridges, whisk with a soft-bristled mushroom brush; do not rinse them, as they readily absorb water. If fresh morels are not available, substitute any other flavorful, fresh wild or cultivated mushrooms. Accompany with wilted spring greens *(recipe on page 97)*, if you like.

IN A SMALL BOWL, combine the boiling water and the dried morels. Let cool to room temperature, about 20 minutes. Line a sieve with cheesecloth (muslin) and place over a bowl. Drain the mushrooms in the sieve, then chop them. Reserve the chopped mushrooms and the mushroom liquid separately.

In a frying pan large enough to hold the chops in a single layer without crowding, warm the vegetable oil over medium heat. Add the pork chops and cook, uncovered, for 5 minutes. Turn the chops over and season to taste with salt and pepper. Reduce the heat to medium-low and continue to cook uncovered, turning occasionally, until golden and firm to the touch, 8–9 minutes longer. Transfer the chops to a warmed platter and cover with aluminum foil to keep warm.

In the same pan over medium-high heat, melt the butter. Add the fresh and dried morels (or other mushrooms) and sauté, stirring, until the fresh mushrooms are soft, 3–4 minutes. Transfer the mushrooms to the platter holding the pork to keep warm. Raise the heat to high and add the chicken stock, chopped thyme and reserved mushroom liquid. Cook until reduced by half, 3–4 minutes.

To serve, transfer the chops to warmed individual plates. Divide the sauce and mushrooms evenly among the chops, spooning them over the top. Garnish with thyme sprigs and serve at once. *Serves 6*

Asian Chicken in Ginger-Lemongrass Broth

For the broth:

1 chicken, 3½ lb (1.75 kg), cut into 6 pieces, then skinned

3 qt (3 l) water

1 piece fresh ginger, 2 inches (5 cm) long, cut crosswise into 8 slices

2 lemongrass stalks, ends trimmed, then cut into 1-inch (2.5-cm) lengths

1 carrot, peeled and coarsely chopped

1 yellow onion, coarsely chopped

2 carrots, peeled and cut in half lengthwise, then cut on the diagonal into thin slices

½ daikon, peeled and cut in half lengthwise, then cut on the diagonal into thin slices

¾ lb (375 g) snow peas (mangetouts), ends trimmed, then cut on the diagonal into ½-inch (12-mm) pieces

3 green (spring) onions, cut on the diagonal into thin slices

   salt and freshly ground pepper

Daikon comes from the Japanese words *dai,* meaning "large," and *kon,* or "roots." It looks like a gigantic white icicle, and although it is a member of the turnip family, the flavor is more akin to radish. Here it is paired with other spring ingredients—snow peas, green onions, lemongrass—in a light Asian stew.

TO MAKE THE BROTH, in a large soup pot, combine the chicken pieces, water, ginger, lemongrass, carrot and onion. Place over high heat and bring to a boil, using a skimmer to skim off any foam that forms on the surface. Reduce the heat to low and simmer very gently, skimming as needed, until the chicken falls from the bones, 50–60 minutes. Remove from the heat and let cool for 1 hour. Using a large kitchen spoon, skim off any fat from the top and discard.

Strain the broth through a fine-mesh sieve into a clean saucepan. Remove the pieces of chicken from the sieve and remove the meat from the bones. Tear the meat into 1-inch (2.5-cm) pieces and return them to the broth. Discard the remaining contents of the sieve.

Place the broth over medium heat and bring to a gentle simmer. Add the carrot and daikon slices and simmer until the vegetables are tender, about 7 minutes. Add the snow peas and green onions and continue to simmer until tender, about 2 minutes longer. Season to taste with salt and pepper.

Ladle into warmed bowls and serve hot. *Serves 6*

The awakened heart can sense spring in the air when there is
no visible suggestion in calendar or frosted earth…

—Hannah Rion

Spinach and Bacon Soufflé

1	teaspoon olive oil
3	slices bacon, 3 oz (90 g), cut into ½-inch (12-mm) squares
⅓	cup (1½ oz/45 g) freshly grated Parmesan cheese
2	tablespoons unsalted butter
1	yellow onion, diced
6	tablespoons (2 oz/60 g) all-purpose (plain) flour
2	cups (16 fl oz/500 ml) milk
5	egg yolks
	salt and freshly ground pepper
6	egg whites, at room temperature
1½	cups (6 oz/185 g) lightly packed shredded Gruyère cheese
2	cups (2 oz/60 g) lightly packed baby spinach leaves or tender larger leaves, torn into pieces, carefully rinsed and dried

Although spinach is sold in markets year-round, its prime season is early spring. It is when you are most likely to find baby leaves, which some growers market already washed and bagged.

IN A FRYING PAN over medium heat, warm the olive oil. Add the bacon and cook, stirring occasionally, until lightly golden and crisp and all the fat is rendered, 6–8 minutes. Using a slotted spoon, transfer to paper towels to drain.

Meanwhile, preheat an oven to 450°F (230°C). Butter a 2-qt (2-l) soufflé dish and dust with half of the Parmesan cheese. Measure out a sheet of aluminum foil long enough to encircle the soufflé dish with an extra 2 inches (5 cm) left over and fold it in half lengthwise. Butter one side of the foil. Wrap it, butter side in, around the soufflé dish, positioning it so that it stands 2 inches (5 cm) above the rim of the dish. Secure in place with kitchen string.

In a saucepan over medium-low heat, melt the 2 tablespoons butter. Add the onion and sauté, stirring occasionally, until soft, about 10 minutes. Stir in the flour and cook, stirring constantly, for 2 minutes, allowing the mixture to bubble. Meanwhile, pour the milk into a saucepan over medium heat and bring it to just below a boil. Remove the onions from the heat and gradually whisk in the hot milk. Return to medium-low heat and cook, stirring constantly with a wooden spoon, until thick and smooth, 2–3 minutes. Transfer to a large bowl and stir in the bacon. Add the egg yolks, one at a time, stirring well after each addition. Season with salt and pepper and set aside.

In a bowl, beat the egg whites until stiff peaks form. Using a rubber spatula, fold half of the whites into the yolk mixture to lighten it. Top with the Gruyère, the remaining whites and the spinach and fold in just until no white drifts remain. Do not overmix. Pour into the prepared soufflé dish. Sprinkle the remaining Parmesan evenly over the top.

Bake until the top is golden and the center no longer quivers when the dish is shaken, 35–45 minutes. Remove the foil and serve immediately. *Serves 4*

The guests are met, the feast is set:
May'st hear the merry din.

—Samuel Taylor Coleridge

Baked Ham with Ginger-Rum Glaze

½ **partially boned country-style cured ham such as a Virginia ham, 6–7 lb (3–3.5 kg)**

30 **whole cloves**

¼ **cup (2 fl oz/60 ml) fresh orange juice**

3 **tablespoons maple syrup**

3 **tablespoons firmly packed brown sugar**

¼ **cup (1½ oz/15 g) preserved ginger in syrup or crystallized ginger**

¼ **cup (2 fl oz/60 ml) light or dark rum**

There is no better centerpiece for the Easter table than an old-fashioned country ham punctuated with cloves and glazed to a rich mahogany brown. The mix of sweet and salty flavors is particularly pleasing. Always seek out the best-quality ham you can find, asking at the butcher shop or delicatessen for one that has been dry-cured with salt and sugar and lightly smoked.

RINSE THE HAM well in several changes of cold water. Place in a large bowl, add water to cover and refrigerate overnight.

Remove the ham from the water and discard the water. Pat dry with paper towels. Using a sharp knife, remove the skin and slice off enough fat so that a layer only ⅓ inch (9 mm) thick remains. Score the ham fat with criss-crosses to form a diamond pattern. Stick a clove in the center of each diamond.

Preheat an oven to 325°F (165°C).

In a small saucepan over high heat, combine the orange juice, maple syrup, brown sugar and ginger and stir until the sugar dissolves, about 1 minute. Add the rum and transfer the mixture to a blender. Blend on high speed to form a smooth glaze. Brush the surface of the ham with some of the glaze and place the ham on a rack in a roasting pan.

Place the pan in the oven and bake, basting every 30 minutes with some of the remaining glaze, until the ham is golden brown and a thick glaze has formed on the surface, 2–2½ hours. Remove from the oven, cover with aluminum foil and let rest for 15 minutes before carving.

To serve, cut the ham into slices and arrange on a warmed platter or individual plates. Serve at once. *Serves 8*

Everything is fruit to me that your seasons bring, Nature.

—Marcus Aurelius Antoninus

Roasted Cornish Hens with Rhubarb Chutney

For the rhubarb chutney:

¾   **cup (6 fl oz/180 ml) red wine vinegar**

⅛   **teaspoon ground cloves**

¼   **teaspoon ground ginger**

½   **cup (4 oz/125 g) sugar**

½   **cup (3 oz/90 g) golden raisins (sultanas)**

1¼   **lb (625 g) rhubarb, trimmed and cut into 1-inch (2.5-cm) pieces**

½   **cup (4 fl oz/125 ml) boiling water**

For the Cornish hens:

6   **Cornish game hens, about 1 lb (500 g) each, halved**

   salt and freshly ground pepper

1½   **tablespoons unsalted butter, melted**

Each of these flavorful 1-lb (500-g) hens, also known as Rock Cornish game hens, provides a perfect serving for one. Rhubarb, available from late winter to early summer, provides a wonderfully tangy sauce; take care to discard any leaves from the stalks, as they are toxic.

TO MAKE THE CHUTNEY, in a saucepan, combine the vinegar, cloves, ginger, sugar and raisins. Bring to a boil, reduce the heat to medium-low and simmer, uncovered, until the raisins soften, about 5 minutes. Add the rhubarb and boiling water. Continue to cook, stirring occasionally, until the rhubarb is soft, about 20 minutes. If any liquid still remains, simmer over high heat until it almost evaporates. Transfer the chutney to a bowl and let cool.

To prepare the hens, preheat an oven to 500°F (260°C). Rinse the hen halves well, then pat dry with paper towels. Sprinkle on all sides with salt and pepper. Place the hen halves, skin side up, in a single layer in a roasting pan. Brush the hens lightly with some of the melted butter. Roast the hens, basting with the remaining butter and the pan juices after about 12 minutes, until they are golden and the juices run clear when a thigh is pierced, about 25 minutes total. Remove from the oven, cover with aluminum foil and let rest for 10 minutes before serving.

To serve, place 2 hen halves on each warmed individual plate. Spoon the chutney on the side. *Serves 6*

Looking as like…as one pea does like another.

—François Rabelais

Veal Stir-fry with Snow Peas and Snow Pea Shoots

1   **lb (500 g) top round of veal, cut into slices ¼ inch (6 mm) thick**

⅓   **cup (3 fl oz/80 ml) soy sauce**

2   **teaspoons cornstarch (cornflour)**

3   **tablespoons peeled and grated fresh ginger**

6   **cloves garlic, minced**

1   **tablespoon Asian sesame oil**

¼   **cup (2 fl oz/60 ml) unseasoned rice vinegar**

1   **fresh jalapeño chili pepper, seeded and finely diced**

2   **tablespoons vegetable oil, or as needed**

¾   **lb (375 g) snow peas (mange-touts), ends trimmed**

½   **cup (4 fl oz/125 ml) chicken stock or water**

6   **cups (6 oz/185 g) lightly packed snow pea shoots**

Both snow peas and their leafy green shoots are edible. The pods should be harvested when they are flat and crisp, and the peas inside are still smaller than peppercorns.

PLACE EACH SLICE OF VEAL between 2 sheets of plastic wrap or waxed paper. Using a meat pounder, pound to an even ⅛-inch (3-mm) thickness. Cut the veal into strips 1 inch (2.5 cm) wide.

In a bowl, combine the soy sauce, cornstarch, ginger, garlic, sesame oil, vinegar and jalapeño. Mix well. Add the veal, toss to coat evenly, cover and let marinate in the refrigerator for 2 hours.

In a wok or large, deep frying pan over medium-high heat, warm 1 tablespoon of the vegetable oil. Add the snow peas and toss and stir constantly until tender but still crisp, 1–2 minutes. Transfer to a bowl and set aside.

Remove the veal from the marinade and reserve the marinade. Add the remaining 1 tablespoon vegetable oil to the wok or frying pan and place over high heat until the pan is very hot and the oil is rippling. Add half of the veal and toss and stir constantly until pale gold, about 2 minutes. Using a slotted spoon, transfer to the bowl holding the snow peas. Repeat with the remaining veal, adding more oil if needed, and transfer to the bowl.

Reduce the heat to medium and add the reserved marinade and the chicken stock or water to the pan. Cook, stirring, until the liquid thickens slightly, about 1 minute. Return the veal and snow peas to the pan and add the snow pea shoots. Toss and stir until the snow pea shoots wilt, 1–2 minutes.

Transfer to a warmed serving dish and serve immediately. *Serves 6*

As for the garden of mint, the very smell of it
alone recovers and refreshes our spirits,
as the taste stirs up our appetite for meat.

—Pliny the Elder

Roast Leg of Spring Lamb with Mint Sauce

For the lamb:

6   cloves garlic, thinly sliced

1   tablespoon chopped fresh mint

½   teaspoon chopped fresh rosemary

    salt and freshly ground pepper

1   leg of lamb, 5–6 lb (2.5–3 kg), trimmed of excess fat

2   tablespoons olive oil

For the mint sauce:

2   cups (2 oz/60 g) lightly packed fresh mint leaves

½   cup (4 fl oz/125 ml) extra-virgin olive oil

2   tablespoons white wine vinegar

1   large clove garlic, minced

    salt and freshly ground pepper

    fresh mint sprigs

Spring lamb is milk-fed, coming from animals only three to five months old. The meat should be pale pink; anything darker is not true spring lamb, and will lack its perfect tenderness and delicate flavor. Serve this dish when you want a glorious centerpiece for a celebration dinner, garnishing the sliced meat with sprigs of the season's abundant fresh mint.

TO PREPARE THE LAMB, in a small bowl, mix together the garlic, chopped mint, rosemary and salt and pepper to taste. Using a sharp paring knife, make incisions 1 inch (2.5 cm) deep all over the meat and insert the garlic mixture into the slits. Rub the meat evenly with the olive oil.

Position a rack in the bottom of an oven and preheat to 450°F (230°C).

Place the lamb, fat side up, on a rack in a large roasting pan and season with salt and pepper. Roast the lamb for 30 minutes. Turn the lamb over and reduce the heat to 325°F (165°C). Continue to roast until an instant-read thermometer inserted into the thickest part of the leg away from the bone registers 130°–135°F (54°–57°C) for medium-rare, or the meat is pink when cut into with a sharp knife, about 45 minutes.

Meanwhile, make the mint sauce: Place the mint leaves, extra-virgin olive oil, vinegar and garlic in a blender or in a food processor fitted with the metal blade. Process on high speed until smooth. Transfer to a bowl and season to taste with salt and pepper.

When the lamb is done, transfer it to a cutting board; reserve the juices in the pan. Cover the lamb loosely with aluminum foil and let rest for 10 minutes before carving. Using a large spoon, skim the fat from the pan juices and strain the juices through a fine-mesh sieve into the mint sauce. Stir well.

To serve, cut the lamb across the grain into thin slices. Arrange the slices on a warmed platter and garnish with mint sprigs. Pass the mint sauce at the table. *Serves 6–8*

Cold in the earth—and fifteen wild Decembers
From those brown hills have melted into spring.

—Emily Brontë

Artichoke and Leek Lasagna

½   lb (250 g) dried semolina lasagna noodles

2   cups (15 oz/470 g) ricotta cheese

¾   cup (3 oz/90 g) freshly grated Parmesan cheese

     salt and freshly ground pepper

2   tablespoons olive oil

12   baby leeks, including 3 inches (7.5 cm) of green, or 5 large leeks, including 1 inch (2.5 cm) of green, cut into ½-inch (12-mm) dice

     juice of 1 lemon

4   large or 20 baby artichokes

½   cup (4 fl oz/125 ml) water

5   cloves garlic, minced

3   cups (24 fl oz/750 ml) milk

3   tablespoons unsalted butter

¼   cup (1½ oz/45 g) all-purpose (plain) flour

     freshly grated nutmeg

½   lb (250 g) whole-milk mozzarella cheese, shredded

BRING A LARGE POT three-fourths full of salted water to a boil. Add the noodles and cook until al dente, 8–12 minutes. Drain, immerse in cold water to cool, drain again and lay on a baking sheet. Cover with plastic wrap.

In a small bowl, stir together the ricotta, Parmesan and salt and pepper to taste; set aside. In a frying pan over medium-low heat, warm the 2 tablespoons olive oil. Add the leeks and sauté until very soft and lightly golden, about 30 minutes. Transfer to a bowl; set the pan and leeks aside.

Have ready a large bowl of water to which you have added the lemon juice. Cut off the top half of each artichoke and remove the tough outer leaves down to the pale green leaves. Cut off the base of the stems and peel away the dark green outer layer. If using large artichokes, cut in half lengthwise and scoop out the prickly chokes. Cut the artichokes, large or small, lengthwise into thin slices. As each is cut, drop it into the bowl of lemon water.

Drain the artichokes and add to the frying pan along with the ½ cup (4 fl oz/125 ml) water and a large pinch each of salt and pepper. Cover and cook over medium heat until the liquid evaporates and the artichokes are tender, about 15 minutes. Add the garlic and cook for 1 minute. Stir into the leeks. Set aside.

Pour the milk into a saucepan and bring to just below a boil. In another saucepan over medium-high heat, melt the butter. Stir the flour into the butter; cook, stirring, for 2 minutes. Remove from the heat and gradually whisk in the hot milk. Return to medium-low heat and cook, stirring, until thick and smooth, 3–4 minutes. Season to taste with salt, pepper and nutmeg.

Position a rack in the upper part of an oven and preheat to 375°F (190°C). Grease a 9-by-13-inch (23-by-33-cm) baking dish with olive oil. Cover the bottom with a layer of the noodles. Spoon one-third of the ricotta mixture over the noodles. Top with one-third of the leek-artichoke mixture and then one-third of the sauce. Repeat the layering twice. Sprinkle on the mozzarella. Bake until golden and bubbling, 40–50 minutes. Let stand for 15 minutes, then cut into squares to serve. *Serves 8–10*

A solid man of Boston.
A comfortable man with dividends,
And the first salmon and the first green peas.

—Henry Wadsworth Longfellow

Peppered Salmon with Snow Peas and Ginger

1   **lb (500 g) snow peas (mangetouts) or sugar snap peas, ends trimmed**

1   **tablespoon finely ground Sichuan peppercorns, optional**

6   **salmon fillets, each 5–6 oz (155–185 g), skinned**

2   **teaspoons corn oil**

1   **teaspoon Asian sesame oil**

   salt

   freshly ground black pepper, if not using Sichuan peppercorns

6   **green (spring) onions, thinly sliced**

2   **teaspoons peeled and grated fresh ginger**

⅓   **cup (3 fl oz/80 ml) dry sherry**

3   **tablespoons soy sauce**

3   **tablespoons unseasoned rice vinegar**

Snow peas are available year-round, but they are at their most tender and sweet in the spring. The entire legume is edible, which accounts for the French name *mangetout,* meaning "eat it all." These are not to be confused with sugar snap peas, the crisp chubby pods filled with immature peas available at the same time of year. For this recipe, either variety can be used.

BRING A LARGE POT three-fourths full of salted water to a boil. Add the peas and simmer until bright green, about 1 minute. Drain and set aside.

If using the ground Sichuan pepper, sprinkle it on both sides of each salmon fillet, distributing it evenly.

In a wide, nonstick frying pan large enough to hold the salmon in a single layer without crowding, warm the corn oil and sesame oil over medium-high heat. Add the salmon fillets and cook until lightly golden on one side, about 4 minutes. Turn, season with salt and, if the Sichuan pepper has been omitted, with black pepper as well. Continue to cook until lightly golden on the second side and opaque throughout when pierced with a knife, about 4 minutes longer. Transfer the salmon to a warmed platter or individual plates and cover loosely with aluminum foil to keep warm.

Place the same pan over medium-high heat. When it is hot, add the peas, green onions and ginger and toss and stir constantly until the green onions soften, about 1 minute. Add the sherry, soy sauce and vinegar and bring to a boil. Boil until the liquid reduces by one-fourth, 20–30 seconds.

Remove from the heat and pour the vegetables and sauce over and around the salmon. Serve immediately. *Serves 6*

The sea-blooms and the oozy woods which wear
The sapless foliage of the ocean

—Percy Bysshe Shelley

Shrimp Cakes with Jalapeño Tartar Sauce

For the jalapeño tartar sauce:

1   cup (8 fl oz/250 ml) mayonnaise

1   teaspoon Dijon mustard

2   teaspoons fresh lemon juice

¼   cup (1¼ oz/37 g) minced gherkins

1   fresh jalapeño chili pepper, seeded and finely diced

    salt and freshly ground pepper

For the shrimp cakes:

½   cup (4 fl oz/125 ml) bottled clam juice or water

1½ lb (750 g) shrimp (prawns), peeled and deveined

4   tablespoons (2 oz/60 g) unsalted butter, or as needed

1   celery stalk, finely diced

8   green (spring) onions, sliced

1¼ cups (3½ oz/105 g) finely crushed saltine crackers

1   teaspoon hot-pepper sauce

2   eggs, well beaten

⅓   cup (3 fl oz/80 ml) mayonnaise

¼   cup (⅓ oz/10 g) finely snipped fresh chives

    salt and freshly ground pepper

    about 3 cups (6 oz/185 g) fresh bread crumbs

Sweet shrimp are a seafood specialty of the spring months, although 1¼ lb (625 g) bay scallops or cod fillets will give the cakes a similar consistency. Poach them as directed for the shrimp, cooking until opaque at the center. If desired, pass lemon wedges at the table.

TO MAKE THE SAUCE, in a small bowl, combine the mayonnaise, mustard, lemon juice, gherkins and jalapeño and stir to mix well. Season to taste with salt and pepper. Set aside.

To make the shrimp cakes, bring the clam juice or water to a boil in a frying pan. Add the shrimp, reduce the heat to low, cover and simmer for 1 minute. Uncover, stir lightly, re-cover and cook until the shrimp curl and are firm to the touch, about 1 minute longer. Using a slotted spoon, transfer the shrimp to a bowl and let cool slightly, then chop finely and reserve.

In a large frying pan over low heat, melt 2 tablespoons of the butter. Add the celery, cover and cook, stirring occasionally, until soft, about 10 minutes. Add the green onions and cook, stirring occasionally, until soft, about 4 minutes. Transfer to a bowl and let cool. Set the pan aside.

Add the saltines, hot-pepper sauce, eggs, mayonnaise, chives, shrimp and salt and pepper to taste to the celery mixture; mix well. If the mixture is too wet to hold its shape, add bread crumbs as needed (about ½ cup/1 oz/30 g) to absorb the excess moisture. Shape into 12 cakes, each 2–2½ inches (5–6 cm) in diameter and ½ inch (12 mm) thick. Spread the remaining bread crumbs in a shallow bowl and dredge the cakes in them, coating evenly.

In the same frying pan over medium heat, melt the remaining 2 tablespoons butter. Add half of the shrimp cakes and sauté, turning once, until golden on both sides, about 6 minutes total. Transfer to a paper towel-lined plate and keep warm. Sauté the remaining cakes in the same way, adding more butter if needed. *Serves 6*

I wiped away the weeds and foam,
I fetched my sea-born treasures home

—Ralph Waldo Emerson

Parchment-Baked Scallops and Asparagus

1½   **lb (750 g) asparagus spears**

½   **teaspoon grated orange zest**

1   **tablespoon fresh orange juice**

¼   **cup (2 oz/60 g) unsalted butter, at room temperature**

    salt and freshly ground pepper

2   **lb (1 kg) bay scallops**

Baking in parchment is an ideal cooking method for springtime, as it accentuates the flavors of the season's fresh ingredients. These packets can be assembled several hours ahead and refrigerated until you bake them. Salmon or sea scallops can be substituted for the bay scallops, and green (spring) onions, sugar snap peas or snow peas can replace all or some of the asparagus.

PREHEAT AN OVEN to 425°F (220°C).

Cut or snap off the tough stem ends from the asparagus spears and discard. Cut the spears into 1½-inch (4-cm) lengths. Bring a large saucepan three-fourths full of salted water to a boil. Add the asparagus and boil until bright green, about 1 minute. Drain well and set aside.

In a small bowl, using a fork, mash together the orange zest, orange juice, butter and salt and pepper to taste.

Cut out 6 hearts from parchment paper, each one 12 inches (30 cm) high and 12 inches (30 cm) wide at its widest point. Spread the 6 parchment hearts in a single layer on a work surface. Divide the scallops and asparagus evenly among them, placing them on the right half of each heart. Season to taste with salt and pepper and dot with the orange butter. Fold the left half of each heart over the filling and, beginning at one end, fold and crease the edges together securely so no juices will escape. Place in a single layer on a large baking sheet.

Bake until the packets have puffed considerably, 7–10 minutes. Remove from the oven and place on warmed individual plates. Cut open the top of each packet with scissors and serve immediately. *Serves 6*

You can't make an omelet without breaking eggs.

—French Proverb

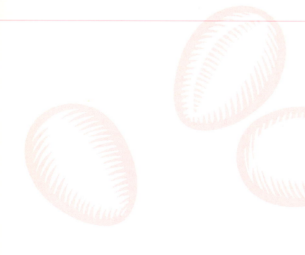

½ cup (4 fl oz/125 ml) bottled clam juice or water

6 oz (185 g) medium shrimp (prawns), peeled and deveined

6 oz (185 g) bay scallops

1 teaspoon saffron threads

6 eggs, separated

¼ cup (1½ oz/45 g) all-purpose (plain) flour

6 oz (185 g) fresh-cooked crab meat

salt and freshly ground pepper

1 tablespoon unsalted butter

Souffléed Shellfish Omelet

Elegant, yet not too complicated, this recipe is ideal for a springtime brunch. Shrimp and bay scallops are at their peak at this time of year; you can also add steamed asparagus, raw baby spinach leaves or blanched sugar snap peas to the omelet, or simply serve them alongside. Accompany with chilled glasses of Champagne topped off with a splash of blood-orange juice.

IN A FRYING PAN over medium heat, bring the clam juice or water to a boil. Add the shrimp and scallops, reduce the heat to low, cover and simmer for 1 minute. Uncover, stir lightly, re-cover and cook until the shrimp curl and the shrimp and scallops are firm to the touch, about 1 minute longer. Using a slotted spoon, transfer the shrimp and scallops to a bowl and let cool. Meanwhile, raise the heat to high and boil until the cooking liquid reduces by half, 20–30 seconds. Place the saffron in a small bowl and pour the reduced cooking liquid over it. Set aside.

Preheat an oven to 375°F (190°C).

In a large bowl, whisk the egg yolks with the flour until smooth. Add the saffron mixture and whisk well. Stir in the shrimp and scallop mixture and the crab until blended. Season to taste with salt and pepper.

In another bowl, using an electric mixer, beat the egg whites until stiff peaks form. Using a rubber spatula, stir one-fourth of the whites into the shellfish mixture to lighten it, then gently fold in the remaining whites just until no white drifts remain. Do not overmix.

Melt the butter in a 10-inch (25-cm) nonstick ovenproof frying pan over medium heat. Tilt the pan to coat the bottom and sides with the butter. Pour the mixture into the pan, spreading it evenly.

Bake until puffed and golden and the center is almost set when the pan is gently shaken, 30–35 minutes. Remove from the oven and serve immediately, spooning the omelet directly from the pan onto individual serving plates.
Serves 4–6

The sea! the sea!

—Xenophon

Panfried Soft-shell Crabs with Lemon

12   **soft-shell crabs**

2   **cups (10 oz/315 g) all-purpose (plain) flour**

½   **teaspoon salt**

¼   **teaspoon freshly ground pepper**

6   **tablespoons (3 oz/90 g) unsalted butter**

     lemon wedges

     fresh flat-leaf (Italian) parsley sprigs

Soft-shell crabs, a wonderful seasonal seafood delicacy, are crabs that have molted their hard shells, leaving just the thin, edible casing of their yet-to-develop new shells. If possible, choose meatier female crabs for this recipe: the tips of their claws are redder, and the "aprons"—the flaps of shell on the bellies—are broader than those of male crabs.

FIRST, CLEAN THE CRABS: Place each crab on its back and twist or cut off the small, triangular apron-shaped shell flap; turn the crab over, lift up the shell and, using your fingers, remove and discard the gray gills. Using scissors, cut off the crab's eyes and mouth. There will be some soft matter just inside this cut. Scoop it out and discard. Rinse the crab and lightly pat it dry with paper towels.

Place the flour in a wide bowl and season it with the salt and pepper. Dredge the crabs lightly in the seasoned flour, tapping off the excess.

Place 2 large frying pans over medium-high heat and add half of the butter to each pan. When it has melted and is foaming, add half of the crabs to each pan in a single layer; do not crowd the pans. Cook until the crabs are reddish brown on the first side, about 3 minutes. Turn them over and cook on the second side until reddish brown, about 3 minutes longer. Using tongs or a slotted spoon, transfer the crabs to paper towels to drain briefly.

Place 2 crabs on each warmed individual plate and garnish with lemon wedges and parsley sprigs. Serve immediately. *Serves 6*

side
dishes

Life is too short to stuff a mushroom.

—Shirley Conran

Wild Mushroom Ragout

1 cup (8 fl oz/250 ml) chicken stock

2 tablespoons chopped fresh flat-leaf (Italian) parsley, plus parsley sprigs for garnish

2 cloves garlic, minced

2 teaspoons unsalted butter

2 teaspoons extra-virgin olive oil

1 lb (500 g) fresh button mushrooms, brushed clean and halved

1 lb (500 g) mixed fresh wild and/or cultivated mushrooms *(see note)*, trimmed, brushed clean and cut into pieces the same size as the button mushroom halves

¼ cup (2 fl oz/60 ml) heavy (double) cream

salt and freshly ground pepper

With spring's arrival comes the appearance in markets of the best young button mushrooms, the smallest variety of cultivated mushrooms, and along with them such wild or specialty varieties as morels, oyster mushrooms and shiitakes. Combine the finest and widest assortment you can find in this rich, flavorful ragout, a lovely complement to steaks or oven-roasted beef.

IN A SMALL SAUCEPAN, bring the chicken stock to a boil and boil until reduced by half, 3–5 minutes. Remove from the heat and set aside.

Combine the chopped parsley and garlic on a cutting board and continue to chop together until very finely minced. Set aside.

In a large frying pan over medium-high heat, melt the butter with the olive oil. Add all the mushrooms and sauté, stirring occasionally, until golden and tender, 5–6 minutes. Add the reduced chicken stock, the cream and the garlic-parsley mixture and simmer over medium heat until reduced by half or until nicely thickened, 3–4 minutes. Season to taste with salt and pepper.

To serve, transfer the mushrooms to a warmed serving dish, garnish with parsley sprigs and serve immediately. *Serves 6*

The delicious scents from earth and leaves,
the glitter of drops on the young green

—Celia Thaxter

Wilted Spring Greens

1	**bunch broccoli rabe, about 1¼ lb (625 g)**
1	**bunch kale, about 1 lb (500 g)**
1	**bunch Swiss chard, about 1 lb (500 g)**
2	**tablespoons extra-virgin olive oil**
2	**tablespoons balsamic vinegar**
2	**cloves garlic, minced**
¼	**teaspoon red pepper flakes**
	salt and freshly ground pepper

An assortment of assertively flavored young, tender spring greens, quickly sautéed in olive oil and aromatically seasoned with balsamic vinegar, garlic and hot red pepper, makes a bold companion to roasted or grilled meat or poultry. Broccoli rabe, also called broccoli raab or rapini, resembles broccoli but has smaller stalks, yellow flowers and a more pungent flavor. You may substitute any of your favorite greens—such as dandelion greens, mâche or arugula (rocket)—for any suggested here.

TRIM AWAY ANY TOUGH stem ends from the broccoli rabe, then cut the stalks crosswise into 2-inch (5-cm) pieces. Trim off the tough kale stems and cut the leaves crosswise into strips 1 inch (2.5 cm) wide. Cut off the white ribs from the Swiss chard and discard. Cut the green leaves crosswise into strips 1 inch (2.5 cm) wide.

In a large frying pan over medium heat, warm the olive oil. Add the broccoli rabe and kale and toss with tongs until they just begin to wilt, about 3 minutes. Add the Swiss chard and continue to toss until the broccoli rabe, kale and Swiss chard have wilted completely but are still bright green, 3–5 minutes longer.

Raise the heat to high and add the balsamic vinegar, garlic and red pepper flakes. Continue to cook, tossing constantly, until the ingredients are well mixed, about 1 minute. Season to taste with salt and pepper.

Transfer to a warmed serving dish and serve immediately. *Serves 6*

An attachment à la Plato for a bashful young potato,
or a not too French French bean!

—W.S. Gilbert

Fennel and New Potato Gratin

1½   lb (750 g) red new potatoes, unpeeled and well scrubbed

3   fennel bulbs

      salt and freshly ground pepper

2   cups (16 fl oz/500 ml) heavy (double) cream, or as needed

1   tablespoon Dijon mustard

¾   cup (3 oz/90 g) freshly grated Parmesan cheese

At their best in early spring, new potatoes are immature tubers measuring only about 1 inch (2.5 cm) in diameter. Their youth gives them thin, soft skins and, because their sugars have not yet turned into starch, a sweet flavor and crisp, waxy texture—all qualities highlighted by this oven-baked recipe that pairs them with bulb fennel. Use feathery fennel fronds as a garnish, if you wish.

CUT THE POTATOES CROSSWISE into slices ¼ inch (6 mm) thick. Bring a large saucepan three-fourths full of salted water to a boil. Add the potatoes and boil until tender yet crisp, 10–12 minutes. Drain well.

Meanwhile, cut off the feathery tops and stems from the fennel bulbs and discard. Trim away any yellowed or bruised outer leaves. Cut in half lengthwise and cut out the tough core portions. Then cut crosswise into slices ¼ inch (6 mm) thick.

Bring a large saucepan three-fourths full of salted water to a boil. Add the fennel and boil until tender, 5–10 minutes. Drain well.

Position a rack in the upper part of an oven and preheat to 375°F (190°C). Butter a 9-by-13-inch (23-by-33-cm) baking dish.

Arrange a row of fennel slices along one short end of the prepared baking dish. Arrange a row of potato slices slightly overlapping the fennel. Continue to form overlapping rows of the fennel and potato slices until the vegetables are used up and the dish is filled. Season to taste with salt and pepper. In a bowl, whisk together 2 cups (16 fl oz/500 ml) cream and the mustard. Pour as much of the cream mixture as needed over the fennel and potatoes to bring the liquid almost level with the vegetables. If the liquid is not deep enough, add more cream as needed. Sprinkle the cheese evenly over the top.

Bake until most of the cream has been absorbed and the top is golden, 30–40 minutes. Remove from the oven and serve immediately. *Serves 6*

On the first warm day of spring I dig my fingers deep into the soft earth. I can feel its energy, and my spirits soar.

—Helen Hayes

Roasted Red and Yellow Beets with Balsamic Glaze

1½ **lb (750 g) red beets, with greens attached** (*see note*)

1½ **lb (750 g) yellow beets, with greens attached** (*see note*)

2 **tablespoons olive oil**

¼ **cup (2 fl oz/60 ml) water**

½ **cup (4 fl oz/125 ml) balsamic vinegar**

3 **tablespoons firmly packed brown sugar**

salt and freshly ground pepper

Most beet varieties are available in markets in late spring. Although the most common type sold are deep garnet-red, you'll also find golden beets and even ones with concentric red and white stripes reminiscent of a candy cane. To insure freshness and tenderness, choose small or medium beets with their greens still attached. Remove the greens as soon as you get home, as they will leach moisture from the roots if stored intact over long periods. Garnish the dish with fresh parsley sprigs, if you like.

PREHEAT AN OVEN to 400°F (200°C).

Trim off the beet greens and reserve for another use. Rinse the beets well, but do not peel, and place in a shallow baking dish. In a small bowl, stir together the olive oil and water. Pour the mixture over the beets and toss to coat them completely.

Cover with aluminum foil and bake until the beets are tender when pierced with a skewer, 45–55 minutes. Remove from the oven, uncover and let cool for 10 minutes.

Meanwhile, in a small saucepan, stir together the balsamic vinegar and brown sugar. Bring to a boil over medium heat, stirring to dissolve the sugar. Boil until reduced by one-third, about 10 seconds. Remove from the heat.

Peel the beets by slipping off the skins, then cut them crosswise into thin slices. Place the sliced beets in a warmed serving bowl and drizzle with the balsamic glaze. Season to taste with salt and pepper, toss to coat and serve immediately. *Serves 6*

See, where she comes apparell'd
like the spring.

—William Shakespeare

Baked Pancetta-Wrapped Endive

18 paper-thin slices pancetta,
     6 oz (185 g) total weight

9   heads Belgian endive
     (chicory/witloof), 1½–2 lb
     (750 g–1 kg)

4   tablespoons (2 fl oz/60 ml)
     fresh lemon juice

3   tablespoons extra-virgin
     olive oil

     salt and freshly ground
     pepper

1   clove garlic, minced

     lemon wedges

Belgian endives, prized for their refreshing crispness and sharp flavor, would be overwhelmingly bitter were it not for the labor-intensive cultivation method of blanching, in which the heads are grown covered with sand in total darkness to yield plump, pale, mild-tasting shoots. Endive is at its peak from late autumn to mid-spring. This dish works equally well served plain as a flavorful side dish or nestled on a bed of frisée as a simple first course.

UNCURL EACH PANCETTA SLICE so that it forms a long strip, and cut each piece crosswise to form 2 equal pieces. Trim the stem end of each endive, being careful not to separate the leaves, and cut lengthwise into quarters.

Position a rack in the upper part of an oven and preheat to 400°F (200°C).

Bring a large pot three-fourths full of salted water to a boil. Add 3 tablespoons of the lemon juice and the endive quarters and cook for 1 minute. Using a slotted spoon, transfer the endive quarters to paper towels to drain, then place in a bowl and drizzle with 1 tablespoon of the olive oil. Toss well and season to taste with pepper.

Working with 1 endive quarter at a time, wrap a piece of pancetta around it, encircling it in a spiral pattern. Arrange the wrapped endives in a single layer in a 9-by-13-inch (23-by-33-cm) baking dish, allowing ample space between them. Bake until the endives are tender when pierced with a knife and the pancetta begins to crisp on the edges, about 15 minutes.

Meanwhile, in a small bowl, whisk together the remaining 1 tablespoon lemon juice and 2 tablespoons olive oil and the garlic. Season to taste with salt and pepper.

To serve, place the endive quarters on a warmed platter and drizzle with the vinaigrette. Serve hot or warm, garnished with lemon wedges. *Serves 6*

desserts

*Doubtless God could have made a better fruit
than the strawberry, but doubtless, God never did.*

—William Butler

Rhubarb and Strawberry Crisp

For the crisp topping:

¾ cup (3 oz/90 g) pecan halves

1½ cups (7½ oz/235 g) all-purpose (plain) flour

½ cup (3½ oz/105 g) firmly
packed brown sugar

1½ teaspoons grated orange zest

¼ teaspoon ground nutmeg

½ cup (4 oz/125 g) unsalted
butter, at room temperature

For the fruit filling:

1½ lb (750 g) rhubarb

2 cups (8 oz/250 g) strawberries,
stems removed and halved
lengthwise

3 tablespoons all-purpose
(plain) flour

½ cup (4 oz/125 g) granulated
sugar, or as needed

Over two centuries ago, English cooks first recognized the culinary potential of rhubarb, until then regarded as an ornamental plant. Although actually a hardy perennial vegetable, rhubarb is generally treated as a fruit and often combined with strawberries, which are also harvested in the spring. Be sure to trim off the toxic leaves from the stalks before using. Serve this sprightly crisp à la mode and garnish with long-stemmed fraises des bois, if you like.

TO MAKE THE TOPPING, preheat an oven to 350°F (180°C). Spread the pecans on a baking sheet and place in the oven until lightly toasted and fragrant, 5–7 minutes. Remove from the oven and let cool. Raise the oven temperature to 375°F (190°C).

Place the nuts in a food processor fitted with the metal blade and pulse several times to form ¼-inch (6-mm) pieces. Transfer the nuts to a small bowl and set aside. In another bowl, stir together the flour, brown sugar, orange zest and nutmeg. Add the flour mixture and butter to the food processor and pulse until the mixture just begins to hold together. Add the nuts and pulse 3 or 4 more times until evenly distributed.

To make the filling, trim the tough ends and the leaves from the rhubarb stalks and then cut crosswise into 1-inch (2.5-cm) pieces. Place in a bowl with the strawberries, flour and ½ cup (4 oz/125 g) sugar, adding more sugar if the strawberries are not particularly sweet. Toss until well mixed. Place the fruit in a 2–2½-qt (2–2.5-l) gratin dish or other shallow baking dish and sprinkle the topping evenly over the surface.

Bake until a skewer inserted into the center enters without any resistance and the top is golden and bubbling around the edges, 35–40 minutes. Remove from the oven and let cool for 20 minutes before serving.

To serve, spoon the crisp into individual dishes. *Serves 8*

Blossom by blossom the spring begins

—Algernon Charles Swinburne

Spring Celebration Cake

For the vanilla cake:

6   eggs

1   cup (8 oz/250 g) **granulated sugar**

1   teaspoon **vanilla extract (essence)**

1⅓ cups (5½ oz/170 g) **sifted all-purpose (plain) flour**

    pinch of salt

1   tablespoon **grated lemon zest**

For the lemon curd:

3   **egg yolks**

¼   cup (2 oz/60 g) **granulated sugar**

2   tablespoons **grated lemon zest**

5   tablespoons (2½ fl oz/75 ml) **fresh lemon juice**

3   tablespoons **unsalted butter, cut into 6 equal pieces**

For the lemon sugar syrup:

⅓   cup (3 oz/90 g) **granulated sugar**

⅓   cup (3 fl oz/80 ml) **water**

3   tablespoons **fresh lemon juice**

1   cup (8 fl oz/250 ml) **heavy (double) cream**

2   tablespoons **confectioners' (icing) sugar**

½   teaspoon **vanilla extract**

    sugared violets *(recipe on page 16)*

TO MAKE THE CAKE: Preheat an oven to 350°F (180°C). Butter two 8-inch (20-cm) round cake pans and line the bottoms with parchment paper.

In a bowl, using an electric mixer, beat together the eggs, sugar and vanilla until a stiff ribbon forms that leaves a trail atop the batter when the beater is lifted, about 1 minute. Sift together half of the flour and the pinch of salt over the eggs and sugar. Add the lemon zest and fold the wet and dry ingredients together partially. Sift the remaining flour over the top and fold in until mixed. Pour the batter into the prepared pans, dividing it evenly.

Bake until a skewer inserted into the center of a cake comes out clean and the top springs back when lightly pressed, 30–35 minutes. Transfer to a rack and let cool for 15 minutes. Run a knife blade around the edges of the cakes, invert onto the rack and remove the pans and parchment.

To make the lemon curd, in a heatproof bowl, whisk together the egg yolks, sugar and lemon zest and juice until blended. Place over (not touching) simmering water in a pan and whisk vigorously until the foam disappears and the mixture is very thick, about 10 minutes. Whisk in the butter until melted. Reduce the heat to low and continue to cook, stirring constantly, until very thick, about 5 minutes longer. Remove from the heat and whisk for 2 minutes. Cover with plastic wrap placed directly on the curd; set aside to cool.

To make the sugar syrup, in a saucepan over medium heat, bring the sugar, water and lemon juice to a boil, stirring to dissolve the sugar. Boil for 30 seconds. Remove from the heat and let cool for at least 15 minutes.

Place 1 cake layer, top side up, on a serving plate. Puncture in several places with a fork and drizzle with half of the sugar syrup. Spread the lemon curd evenly onto the cake. Place the second cake layer, top side up, over the first and repeat with the fork and remaining sugar syrup. In a bowl, beat together the cream, confectioners' sugar and vanilla until almost-stiff peaks form. Spread over the top and sides of the cake. Chill for at least 30 minutes or for up to 2 hours. Sprinkle with violets just before serving. *Serves 10*

...from a grove beyond the wall came an
erotic waft of early orange blossom.

—Giuseppe di Lampedusa

Blood Orange and Mango Sherbet

4 large ripe mangoes

3 lb (1.5 kg) blood oranges

about 1 cup (8 oz/240 g) sugar

candied citrus zest *(recipe on page 16)*

Blood oranges are so abundant in Sicily that it is not uncommon to greet each morning with a big glass of their fresh-squeezed juice. Today, they are also propagated in the United States, and are in season from January through late spring. You may substitute limes, lemons (especially the Meyer variety), oranges or grapefruit. For a fanciful presentation, scrape any remaining pulp from the orange halves after juicing, then freeze and use as frosted serving cups.

WORKING WITH 1 MANGO AT A TIME, cut off the flesh from each side of the large, flat pit to form 2 large pieces. Trim any remaining flesh from around the edge of the pit then discard the pit. Using a knife, peel away and discard the skin. Place in a food processor fitted with the metal blade or in a blender.

Finely grate the zest from 2 blood oranges and set aside. Juice all the oranges and strain through a coarse-mesh sieve into the food processor or blender, pushing as much of the pulp through the sieve as possible. Process until smooth. Add the grated zest and process briefly to mix.

Measure the fruit purée; you should have about 4 cups (32 fl oz/1 l). For each 1 cup (8 fl oz/250 ml) fruit purée, measure out ¼ cup (2 oz/60 g) sugar. To dissolve the sugar, pour approximately one-fourth of the fruit purée into a small saucepan and add the measured sugar. Stir well and place over medium-high heat, stirring constantly, until the sugar dissolves, 3–4 minutes. Pour the contents of the saucepan back into the fruit purée and stir to distribute evenly. Cover and place in the refrigerator until well chilled, about 2 hours.

Freeze in an ice cream maker according to the manufacturer's instructions. To serve, spoon into individual serving dishes and garnish with candied citrus zest. *Serves 6*

I felt suddenly, as I rose again, a bitter-sweet fragrance of almonds steal towards me from the hawthorn-blossom…

—Marcel Proust

Marzipan Cake

1	cup (8 oz/250 g) sugar
6	oz (185 g) marzipan
¾	cup (6 oz/185 g) unsalted butter, at room temperature
¼	teaspoon almond extract (essence)
5	eggs, at room temperature
¾	cup (4 oz/125 g) plus 2 tablespoons all-purpose (plain) flour
1¼	teaspoons baking powder
¼	teaspoon salt

In countries where almonds are grown, the harvest begins in late spring, and the fresh nuts are much prized. Drying, however, makes this versatile nut available year-round, and the almond-sugar paste known as marzipan extends the range of its uses. Top slices of this moist cake with fresh strawberries and softly whipped cream, or offer it plain with tea or coffee.

PREHEAT AN OVEN to 350°F (180°C). Butter an 8½-by-4½-by-2½-inch (21-by-11-by-6-cm) loaf pan and then dust with flour. Tap out the excess flour.

Using an electric mixer or a food processor fitted with the metal blade, pulverize together the sugar and marzipan until the mixture is in fine pieces. If a food processor was used, transfer the mixture to a large bowl. Add the butter and almond extract and mix until light and fluffy, 1–2 minutes. Add the eggs, one at a time, beating well after each addition until thoroughly combined. Sift together the flour, baking powder and salt over the egg mixture and beat in just until thoroughly blended.

Pour the batter into the prepared pan. Bake until a toothpick inserted into the center comes out clean and the top springs back when lightly pressed, about 1¼ hours. Transfer the pan to a rack and let cool for 15 minutes. Run a knife blade around the edge of the cake and invert onto the rack. Lift off the pan and cool the cake upright on the rack for at least 30 minutes before serving. *Serves 8–10*

O! it came o'er my ear like the sweet sound
That breathes upon a bank of violets,
Stealing and giving odor!

—William Shakespeare

Lemon Cloud Tart

For the short-crust tart shell:

1½ cups (7½ oz/235 g) all-purpose (plain) flour

1½ tablespoons sugar

pinch of salt

¾ cup (6 oz/185 g) unsalted butter, out of the refrigerator for 15 minutes, cut into pieces

about 1½ tablespoons water

For the lemon filling:

4 egg yolks

⅓ cup (3 oz/90 g) sugar

3 tablespoons grated lemon zest

juice of 2 lemons

3 tablespoons unsalted butter, melted

⅓ cup (1½ oz/45 g) lightly toasted and finely ground blanched almonds

For the meringue:

3 egg whites, at room temp-erature

¾ cup (6 oz/185 g) sugar

½ teaspoon vanilla extract (essence)

sugared violets or other spring blossoms *(recipe on page 16),* optional

Lemon meringue pie is a favorite recipe of spring, when lemons and eggs are in abundance. This recipe introduces an intriguing variation.

TO MAKE THE TART SHELL, in a food processor fitted with the metal blade, combine the flour, sugar and salt, and pulse a few times to mix. Add the butter and pulse until the mixture resembles coarse meal. With the motor running, add water as needed to bind the ingredients. Gather into a ball, flatten into a disk 6 inches (15 cm) in diameter and wrap in plastic wrap. Refrigerate for 30 minutes.

Preheat an oven to 400°F (200°C). Gently press the pastry into the bottom and sides of a 9-inch (23-cm) tart pan with a removable bottom, forming a slightly thicker layer on the sides. Place the shell in the freezer for 30 minutes.

Line the pastry with aluminum foil and fill with pie weights. Bake for 10 minutes. Remove the weights and foil and reduce the temperature to 375°F (190°C). Continue to bake until lightly golden, 15–20 minutes longer.

Meanwhile, make the filling: In a bowl, using an electric mixer, beat together the egg yolks and sugar until they form a stiff ribbon that leaves a trail atop the batter when the beater is lifted, about 1 minute. Stir in the lemon zest and juice, then the melted butter and finally the ground almonds.

Remove the tart shell from the oven and immediately pour the filling into it. Return it to the oven and bake until a skewer inserted into the center comes out clean, 20–30 minutes. Transfer to a rack and let cool completely.

Raise the oven temperature to 450°F (230°C). To make the meringue, using an electric mixer, beat the egg whites until soft peaks form. Slowly add the sugar while continuing to beat until stiff peaks form. Fold in the vanilla. Spoon the meringue over the cooled filling, spreading it to the edges of the pastry and forming peaks.

Bake until the meringue is golden brown, about 7 minutes. Let cool and chill until set, about 1 hour. Garnish each serving with sugared blossoms, if desired. Serve chilled. *Serves 8*

Let my beloved come to his garden,
And eat its choicest fruits.

—Song of Solomon

For the sponge cake:

6	eggs, separated, at room temperature
¾	cup (6 oz/185 g) sugar
1	teaspoon vanilla extract (essence)
⅔	cup (3½ oz/105 g) all-purpose (plain) flour
⅓	cup (1½ oz/45 g) cake (soft-wheat) flour
	pinch of salt
¾	cup (6 fl oz/180 ml) heavy (double) cream
6	egg yolks
1	cup (8 oz/240 g) sugar
½	cup (4 fl oz/125 ml) orange liqueur such as Grand Marnier or Mandarin Napoleon
3	cups (12 oz/375 g) strawberries, hulled
4	mangoes, peeled and pitted
½	cup (4 fl oz/125 ml) pineapple juice
¼	cup (2 fl oz/60 ml) dark rum
	seeds and juice from 6 passion fruits

Tropical Fruit Trifle

TO MAKE THE SPONGE CAKE, preheat an oven to 350°F (180°C). Butter and lightly flour an 11½-by-17½-inch (28.5-by-44-cm) jelly-roll pan. Line the bottom with parchment paper. In a bowl, using an electric mixer, beat together the egg yolks, sugar and vanilla until thick and tripled in volume, about 1 minute. Sift half of the flours and salt over the eggs and sugar and, using a rubber spatula, fold together partially. Sift the remaining flour mixture over the top and fold in until mixed. In another bowl, beat the egg whites to soft peaks. Fold half of the whites into the batter to lighten it. Then fold in the remaining whites. Spread the batter evenly into the prepared pan.

Bake until the top springs back when lightly pressed, about 15 minutes. Let cool in the pan on a rack. Invert onto the rack and remove the pan and parchment. Cut into 4 equal sections and let stand until dry, 12–24 hours.

In a bowl, beat the cream to soft peaks. Cover and refrigerate.

Fill a bowl one-fourth full with ice water. In a heatproof bowl, combine the egg yolks, 6 tablespoons (3 oz/90 g) of the sugar and the liqueur. Place over (not touching) simmering water in a pan; whisk vigorously until tripled in volume and soft mounds form, about 5 minutes. Nest the bowl in the ice water; whisk until cold. Fold in the whipped cream, cover and refrigerate.

In a blender, combine the strawberries and 5 tablespoons (2½ oz/75 g) of the remaining sugar; purée until smooth. Strain into a bowl; set aside. Put the mangoes and the remaining 5 tablespoons (2½ oz/75 g) sugar in the blender; purée until smooth. Strain into another bowl; set aside.

To assemble the trifle, spread one-fourth of the strawberry purée over the bottom of a 2½-qt (2.5-l) straight-sided glass bowl. Trim 1 of the cake sections to fit in the bowl and place it and the trimmed pieces over the purée. In a small bowl, combine the pineapple juice and rum and sprinkle 3 tablespoons of the mixture over the cake. Drizzle with one-fourth of the passion fruit seeds and juice, then with one-fourth of the mango purée, and top with one-fourth of the orange cream. Repeat the layering three more times, starting with the berry purée. Cover and refrigerate for at least 8 hours before serving. *Serves 10*

Sweet spring full of sweet days and roses,
A box where sweets compacted lie.

—George Herbert

Black Bottom Banana Cream Pie

For the pastry shell:

1½ cups (7½ oz/235 g) all-purpose (plain) flour

½ teaspoon salt

1 tablespoon granulated sugar

½ cup (4 oz/125 g) chilled unsalted butter

3 tablespoons vegetable shortening

3 tablespoons ice water

For the banana cream filling:

3 eggs

½ cup (4 oz/125 g) granulated sugar

pinch of salt

3 tablespoons cornstarch (cornflour)

2 cups (16 fl oz/500 ml) milk

3 tablespoons unsalted butter

1½ teaspoons vanilla extract

2 oz (60 g) European bitter-sweet chocolate, chopped

2¼ cups (18 fl oz/560 ml) heavy (double) cream

4 small, ripe yet firm bananas

½ cup (4 fl oz/125 ml) fresh orange juice

1 tablespoon confectioners' (icing) sugar

dried banana chips and fresh berries, optional

TO MAKE THE PASTRY SHELL, in a large bowl, stir together the flour, salt and sugar. Make a well in the center. Cut the butter and shortening into pieces, add to the well, and rub together with your fingertips to form large, flat pieces. Sprinkle on the water and mix with a fork until the mixture just holds together. Gather into a rough ball. Wrap in plastic wrap and chill for 2 hours.

Preheat an oven to 375°F (190°C). On a floured surface, roll out the dough into a 12-inch (30-cm) round. Transfer to a 9-inch (23-cm) pie pan or tart pan with a removable bottom and press in gently. Trim the edges even with the pan rim and, if using a pie pan, flute decoratively. Prick the bottom and the sides with a fork. Place in the freezer for 10 minutes.

Line the pastry with aluminum foil and fill with pie weights. Bake for 15 minutes. Remove the weights and foil and continue to bake until lightly golden, 10–15 minutes longer. Transfer to a rack and let cool.

To make the filling, in a bowl, whisk together the eggs, granulated sugar and salt. Whisk in the cornstarch. Heat the milk almost to a boil. Whisk the hot milk into the egg mixture and return to the pan. Cook over medium heat, stirring, until thickened, 3–4 minutes. Remove from the heat and stir in the butter and 1 teaspoon of the vanilla. Strain through a sieve into a bowl and cover with plastic wrap placed directly on the custard; let cool.

In a small saucepan over medium heat, combine the chocolate and ¼ cup (2 fl oz/60 ml) of the cream. Stir until smooth. Let cool completely, stirring occasionally. Pour into the prebaked pastry shell; refrigerate for 10 minutes.

Cut the bananas crosswise into slices ½ inch (12 mm) thick. Place in a bowl and toss with the orange juice. Drain well and pat dry with paper towels. Stir into the vanilla custard, then pour into the pastry shell and smooth the top.

In a bowl, beat the remaining 2 cups (16 fl oz/500 ml) cream with the confectioners' sugar and the remaining ½ teaspoon vanilla until almost stiff. Decoratively top the pie with the cream. Sprinkle with banana chips and berries, if desired. Chill for 1 hour before serving. *Serves 8*

We...waded in the tepid water under the lime trees,
and waited for the night to bring out the smell of the jasmine.

—Santha Rama Rau

Lemon-Lime Cheesecake

For the crust:

3   tablespoons granulated sugar

¼   cup (2 oz/60 g) unsalted
     butter, at room temperature

1½   teaspoons grated lemon zest

1   egg yolk

1   cup (5 oz/155 g) all-purpose
     (plain) flour

¼   teaspoon baking powder

     pinch of salt

For the lemon-lime filling:

1¼   lb (625 g) cream cheese, at
     room temperature

¾   cup (6 oz/185 g) granulated
     sugar

¾   cup (6 fl oz/180 ml) sour
     cream

1   tablespoon grated lemon zest

1   tablespoon grated lime zest

2   tablespoons fresh lemon
     juice

2   tablespoons fresh lime juice

4   eggs

If you like, make a glaze for this rich dessert by whisking together 1 table-spoon fresh lemon juice and 3 tablespoons sifted confectioners' (icing) sugar. Brush the glaze over the cake just before serving. Arrange candied citrus zest *(recipe on page 16)* on the top.

PREHEAT AN OVEN to 325°F (165°C). Butter the bottom of a 9-inch (23-cm) springform cake pan and line the bottom with parchment paper cut to fit precisely. Wrap aluminum foil around the outside of the pan to prevent seepage during baking.

To make the crust, in a food processor fitted with the metal blade, combine the sugar and butter and process until light and fluffy. Add the lemon zest and yolk and process until smooth. In a bowl, sift together the flour, baking powder and salt and add to the processor. Pulse a few times until mixed but still crumbly.

Gather the dough together and press it evenly over the bottom of the prepared pan. Bake until golden, 25–30 minutes. Let cool on a rack.

Meanwhile, make the filling: Using an electric mixer, beat the cream cheese on low speed until smooth, about 30 seconds. Slowly add the sugar, beating for an additional 30 seconds. Add the sour cream and lemon and lime zest and juice and beat for another 30 seconds. Add the eggs, one at a time, beating after each addition only until each has been absorbed. Scrape down the sides of the bowl and beat for 10 seconds longer.

Pour the filling over the crust and place the pan inside a larger baking pan. Pour hot water into the larger pan to a depth of ½ inch (12 mm). Bake until golden brown and firm to the touch, 1–1¼ hours. Transfer the cheesecake pan to a rack and let cool. Cover with foil and chill overnight.

To serve, remove the foil and pan sides and carefully slide the cake off the pan bottom onto a serving plate. Serve chilled, cut into wedges. *Serves 12*

'Long about knee-deep in June,
'Bout the time strawberries melts
On the vine.

—James Whitcomb Riley

White Chocolate Mousse with Strawberries

2   **cups (8 oz/240 g) strawberries, stems removed**

¼   **cup (2 oz/60 g) sugar**

1   **tablespoon kirsch or framboise**

6   **oz (185 g) white chocolate, finely chopped**

¼   **cup (2 fl oz/60 ml) milk, warmed**

1   **cup (8 fl oz/250 ml) heavy (double) cream**

2   **egg whites, at room temperature**

     pinch of cream of tartar

¾   **teaspoon vanilla extract (essence)**

Strawberries are members of the rose family and have long grown wild in Europe and the Americas. Today, they are cultivated almost year-round, although they are sweetest and juiciest during their peak, from April to June. White chocolate marries especially well with their wonderful flavor.

IN A BLENDER or in a food processor fitted with the metal blade, combine 1½ cups (6 oz/180 g) of the strawberries with the sugar. Purée until smooth. Strain through a fine-mesh sieve into a bowl. Add the kirsch or framboise and stir to mix. Cut the remaining ½ cup (2 oz/60 g) strawberries lengthwise into thin slices and stir into the purée. Set aside.

Place the chocolate in a heatproof bowl set over a pan of gently simmering water; do not allow the bowl to touch the water. Heat the chocolate, stirring occasionally, until it is melted and smooth and registers 140°F (60°C) on an instant-read thermometer. Gradually add the warm milk to the chocolate, stirring constantly until smooth. Remove the bowl from the pan of water and let the mixture cool until it is almost at room temperature.

In a bowl, using an electric mixer on high speed, beat the cream just until soft peaks form. In another bowl, using clean beaters, beat together the egg whites and cream of tartar on high speed until stiff peaks form. Using a rubber spatula, fold half of the whites into the chocolate mixture to lighten it. Fold the remaining whites, whipped cream and vanilla into the chocolate mixture just until combined and no white drifts remain. Do not overmix. (At this point, you may cover and refrigerate the mousse for up to 1 day.)

To serve, spoon about half of the mousse into 6 parfait glasses, half filling each glass. Top with the strawberry sauce, again using about half and dividing it equally. Repeat with the remaining mousse and strawberry sauce. *Serves 6*

Ah, you flavor everything; you are the vanilla of society.

—Sydney Smith

Warm Pineapple Compote

1 pineapple, about 4 lb (2 kg)

¼ cup (2 fl oz/60 ml) dark rum

½ cup (3 oz/90 g) golden raisins (sultanas)

3 tablespoons unsalted butter

¼ cup (2 oz/60 g) firmly packed dark brown sugar

½ cup (4 fl oz/125 ml) pineapple juice

Native to Central and South America, the pineapple is a symbol of hospitality. Pineapples are available year-round with peak season from March through June. This warm compote is also delicious served with pound cake and softly whipped cream or atop a generous scoop of vanilla ice cream.

GRASP THE LEAFY TOP of the pineapple and twist it off. Using a sharp knife, cut off the top just below the crown. Cut a slice ½ inch (12 mm) thick off the bottom. Place the pineapple upright and, using a sharp knife, cut off the peel in vertical strips. Using the knife tip, cut out the round "eyes" on the pineapple sides. Cut the pineapple lengthwise into quarters and cut out the core. Cut each quarter in half lengthwise, then cut each piece crosswise into slices ½ inch (12 mm) thick.

In a saucepan over medium heat, heat the rum until bubbles appear along the pan edges, about 1 minute. Add the raisins, stir once or twice and remove from the heat. Set aside, stirring occasionally, until cool, about 30 minutes. Drain the raisins, reserving the rum and raisins separately.

In a large frying pan over high heat, melt 1 tablespoon of the butter. When hot, add half of the pineapple slices and cook until golden on the first side, about 2 minutes. Turn over the pineapple slices and cook on the second side until golden, about 2 minutes longer. Using a slotted spoon, transfer to a plate. Repeat with the remaining pineapple and another tablespoon of the butter and set aside with the first batch. Wash and dry the pan.

Place the pan over medium-high heat and add the remaining 1 tablespoon butter. When it melts, add the brown sugar and heat, stirring, until the sugar melts, 1–2 minutes. Add the pineapple juice and cook until reduced by half, 1–2 minutes. Add the raisins, 1 tablespoon of the reserved rum and the pineapple. Mix together gently and cook until the pineapple is heated through, 1–2 minutes.

To serve, spoon into individual serving bowls and serve at once. *Serves 6*

It's food too fine for angels; yet come, take
And eat thy fill! It's Heaven's sugar cake.

—Edward Taylor

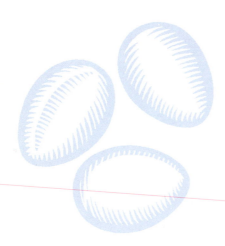

¾   cup (4 oz/125 g) blanched
    almonds

2   cups (6 oz/185 g) unsweetened
    flaked dried coconut

2   egg whites, at room temper-
    ature

¼   teaspoon cream of tartar

¾   cup (6 oz/185 g) sugar

Coconut Macaroons

These rich, chewy cookies are inspired by a recipe from Lindsey Shere, the pastry chef at Chez Panisse in Berkeley, California, and the author of *Chez Panisse Desserts*. Served alongside chocolate eggs and other springtime confections, they are the perfect conclusion to an Easter brunch. Drizzle them with melted chocolate before serving, if you like.

PREHEAT AN OVEN to 350°F (180°C). Spread the almonds on a baking sheet and place in the oven until lightly toasted and fragrant, 5–7 minutes. Remove from the oven, let cool and chop finely. Set aside.

Raise the oven temperature to 375°F (190°C). Line the same baking sheet with parchment paper.

Spread the coconut on the parchment-lined baking sheet and bake, stirring often, until golden, 5–10 minutes. Remove from the oven and transfer to a bowl to cool. Reduce the oven temperature to 325°F (165°C). Leave the parchment paper on the baking sheet.

In another bowl, combine the egg whites and cream of tartar. Using an electric mixer on high speed, beat until stiff peaks form. Gradually add the sugar and continue beating until stiff peaks form again. Using a rubber spatula, gently fold in the nuts and coconut, distributing them as evenly as you can. Be careful not to deflate the mixture.

For each cookie, scoop up about 1 teaspoon of the egg white mixture and gently shape it into a 1-inch (2.5-cm) ball with your fingers. Place the balls on the parchment-lined baking sheet, spacing them about 1 inch (2.5 cm) apart.

Bake until lightly golden, 14–16 minutes. Remove from the oven, transfer to a rack and let cool. Store in an airtight container at room temperature for up to 2 days. *Makes about 3½ dozen*

index

acknowledgments

The following kindly lent props for photography: The Gardener, Berkeley, CA; Fillamento, San Francisco, CA;
American Rag, San Francisco, CA; Jon and Deahn Chaney; Chuck Williams; Williams-Sonoma and Pottery Barn.
The publishers would also like to thank Sarah Lemas, Ruth Jacobsen, Sherilyn Hovind and Ken DellaPenta for their editorial assistance.
Thanks also goes to Penina and Michelle Syracuse for surfaces used in photography, and to
Joanne Lees, Jean Tenanes and Paul Weir for their support to the author.